Political Anthropology Volume 3

RELIGION AND POLITICS

Political Anthropology Volume 3

RELIGION AND POLITICS

Edited by

Myron J. Aronoff

Transaction Books
New Brunswick (U.S.A.) and London (U.K.)

ISSN: 0732-1228
ISBN: 0-87855-459-9 (cloth): 0-87855-977-9 (paper)
Printed in the United States of America

CONTENTS

Introduction

Myron J. Aronoff

Religion and Politics have been inextricably interrelated since the dawn of human culture and civilization. Yet the scholarly tradition has tended to reify the dichotomous analytic distinctions made to distinguish between these two dimensions of human activity. The study of non-Western, so called traditional, societies forced scholars to begin to come to terms with the complexity of these interrelationships, and this in turn may lead to a reconsideration of what has been the accepted view of the development of Western civilization. As Horowitz perceptively points out in his essay in this volume, the dualistic approach to the study of religion and politics has been called into question, and is no longer considered to be a cosmic certainty. He argues that the introduction of the focus on culture provides an important new paradigm, a more synthetic approach to understanding the relationship between religion and politics.

The post–World War II "behavioral revolution" in political science resulted in a significant estrangement between contemporary political science and its intellectual roots in classical political theory (or philosophy). Political anthropology is currently reestablishing a dialogue with classical political thought based on their common concern with understanding cultural meanings in and of politics. An excellent example of this new dialogue is illustrated in McWilliams's penetrating analysis of the central importance of the Bible in American political thought and life. He shows that the influence of Scripture on American politics is far more venerable than the activities of fundamentalist groups like the Moral Majority; and that the past biblically based alternative to the liberal tradition differs radically from that proposed by contemporary religious-political American leaders like the Reverend Falwell.

Liebman and Don-Yehiya argue that democratic "visionary" regimes like Israel rely on traditional religious symbols that evoke a "sense of the sacred" in order to mobilize and integrate the society, and to provide legitimacy for the regime and the political system. They analyze the different strategies for transforming and transvaluing traditional symbols in three varieties of civil religion that have been dominant in Israel in different periods. They conclude that Israel's new civil religion is based primarily on a reinterpretation of tradi-

1

tional symbols that have penetrated the present civil religion to a much greater extent than in previous ones.

My own essay focuses on Gush Emunim (bloc of the faithful), a movement that seeks religious ends through political means and justifies unorthodox political tactics by evoking religious authority and sentiments. Gush Emunim is characterized as a charismatic, messianic, religious-political revitalization movement that undergoes a process of institutionalization, differentiation, and incorporation into the ruling Israeli political establishment. The analysis of this case illustrates the inadequacy of a dualistic approach to the study of religion and politics, and illustrates an alternative approach that was published in the introductory essays to the first two volumes in this series.

Unlike Christianity, traditional Judaism and Islam are all-encompassing ways of life that make Western dualistic distinctions between church and state inappropriate. To be sure, at different periods in their respective histories one must differentiate between religious and political offices, institutions, and functions, but not in simple dichotomous terms. Both Judaism in biblical periods and Islam throughout most of its history have lacked the Christian notion of "render unto Caesar...." The prophets provided important authoritative checks on the biblical monarchs. Islamic revitalization movements with "radical" political agendas are posing challenges to regimes throughout the contemporary Middle East.

The revolution in Iran was a spectacular example of the aforementioned phenomenon. Green vividly illustrates the leading role played by the Shia clergy in the countermobilization that successfully overthrew the regime of the Shah. He carefully puts the religious character of the countermobilization in perspective of wider social and political forces. Green's essay is an important contribution to our understanding of the relationship between religious and revolutionary political processes.

Very little is known about the Shia community in Lebanon, which, until recently, had been relatively politically quiescent. Norton's essay is therefore a particularly welcome contribution because it fills an important gap in our knowledge. The belated mobilization of this politically neglected community (in which religious confession defines sociopolitical as well as personal identity) was facilitated by a sense of economic deprivation and disproportionate suffering from Israeli reprisals against PLO raids. The leading Shia cleric in the country, an Iranian-born charismatic imam named Musa al-Sadr founded the modern Shia national movement in Lebanon, which was influenced by events in Iran. His disappearance in Libya made Imam Musa al-Sadr a martyr and a symbol of unity for the divided Lebanese Shia community.

Although all of the contributors to this volume are political scientists (Horowitz and I wear two professional hats—he as a sociologist and I as an anthropologist), the diversity of approaches and methodologies represented in these essays is striking. And yet the essays are unified by more than their common thematic focus. Whereas each case study is analyzed from a different perspective, each explores the role of traditional religious values, symbols, affiliations, and/or leaders in dealing with contemporary sociopolitical realities. Each attempts to analyze the way in which religious traditions help shape the understanding and meaning of contemporary political realities, and how they are reinterpreted and used to accomplish political, as well as religious, goals. These essays illustrate the inadequacy of simplistic distinctions between religion and politics, and suggest more satisfactory ways of approaching the complex nature of the dynamic phenomena with which they deal.

1

Religion, the State, and Politics

Irving Louis Horowitz

The recent literature of political and social science is most impressive in its clear break with formalism. Not more than a decade or two ago the commitment to powerful boundaries between the structure of society and the function of its parts, as represented in the tradition of David Easton in political theory and Talcott Parsons in social theory, was clear-cut. In an odd way, such formalism derived from a classic European model: in Marxian terms, a dualism of base and structure; in Toennies's terms, a distiction between *Gesellschaft* and *Gemeinschaft*; in Durkheimian terms, a gap between the contractual and the organic; in Weberian terms, a perennial struggle between charismatic and rational authority. The entire sweep in political and social theory assumed dualism as not only a mode of analysis but a deep structure of mind.

The metaphysics of dualism has a religious tradition within both Western culture and the Western state. The schism extended much deeper than denominational squabbles, into inherited beliefs: notions of the profane and the sacred, the divine and the material. An entire architectonic of dual realms evolved. Some realms belonged to Caesar; others belonged to the pope. God presumably arranges a harmony of realms that interact in an uncomfortable manner but manage to remain distinct and separate. God becomes purveyor of a system of metaphysical checks and balances.

In Western culture, the Western tradition, we do not grow up with an idea of secularity or religiosity per se but with the idea of a natural and organic dualism of the two. The religious consciousness is said to derive its meaning from its opposite, the political consciousness. Social scientists who operated earlier on in the century took dualist formulations for granted rather than explore them. Evans-Pritchard in political anthropology and Ruth Benedict in cultural anthropology, for example, both understood the world as a cross between the chrysanthemum and the sword. There was an increasing belief that the great dualism in the West, expressed in religious terms, rendering the categories of religion in one area, the categories of the polity in the other, applied to East and West alike. The social scientific community expanded its geographical horizons more readily than its intellectual categories. The great wall separating religion and the polity, in terms of American political theory, was also a separation between the empirical and the theological, the scientific and the religious.

Social science in its "classical epoch" has grown up with these dualisms. We have imbibed them as mother's milk. However, they are finally being called into question. If state building and religion have any meaning, any merit, it is that their dualism has dissolved in a monumental intellectual reconsideration. We no longer believe that the theoretical constructs of earlier periods are necessarily as valid as they once were; if indeed they ever were at all. We may still argue on legalistic, jurisprudential grounds that there should be a distinction between church and state, but we no longer believe that they occupy separate realms; in short, we have broken with an intellectual inheritance. The real rub is that we cannot justify such dualism any longer either to ourselves or to others.

In present circumstances, we have been compelled to readmit a variable that has beclouded everything else in political theory: that everything is the concept of culture. Political anthropology is such an important area not because a sufficient number of people are interested in this particular subject matter to produce a yearbook but because the notion of culture necessarily both threatens and supervenes the notion of social system, on one hand, and the notion of the religious or supernatural order, on the other. The concept of the cultural is sufficiently general, but also sufficiently powerful, as an explanatory variable to upset the great dualism with which we in social science have grown up, and to move us to a higher synthetic ground.

Let me underscore this point: Why is the anthropological tool so useful in understanding societies and policies? Suppose we have a purely structural analysis of systems. Suppose we want to examine, for instance, varieties of totalitarianism. A formal model of organizations might properly draw our attention to a high overlap between Nazi Germany from 1933 to 1945 and Fascist Italy from 1921 to 1943; this is especially so if one looks at the overlaps and similitudes between party organization and administrative bureaucracy in the two countries. One might ask: "What are the characteristics of mobilization under totalitarianism?" The answer is likely to be: There are both high-mobilization societies at the military level and low-mobilization societies at the level of labor or independent organization. If one examines the role of voluntary organizational life and voluntary associations with totalitarian systems, one finds that in both Italian Fascism and German Nazism they are extremely low. One could generate a reasonable Gutmann scale of values about Italy and Germany during their dictatorial periods, and evaluate them as being very close to each other. If one added into this mix the Soviet Union under Stalin, one could further develop a sense of statistically significant correlations among totalitarian systems.

A "sixth sense," if you will, tells us that Italy and Germany are not the same, not even during the Fascist period. As soon as we look for dissimilarities, holding formal, structural elements constant, we enter the realm of the cultural seriously. We are describing Roman Catholicism in Italy vis-à-vis mixed religious systems with a heavy preponderance of Protestantism in Germany. We are describing modes of bureaucratic authority in Germany along Weberian lines, rather than modes of administrative power along Paretan lines in Italy. We are considering people who have a differing sense of appropriate behavior in everyday life—Latin people (so called) vis-à-vis Nordic people (so called). As soon as these distinctions are carefully drawn, we start to address phenomena that social research has not so much analyzed as simply suppressed in the name of avoiding the stereotypical: ranging from national types to personality characteristics.

Political anthropology introduces a range of events with which conventional formalist analysis has not wanted to deal. Social science has evolved essentially within the context of a democratic culture; hence, we are terribly enlightened. We know that Lombroso was morally wrong in trying to identify criminal types in terms of physical characteristics. We know that one cannot, or at least should not, make generalizations about nations and people, cultures and religions. We have converted an unthinking democratic ethos into an intellectual pathos. As a result, our generation of researchers has inherited a crisis in the analytical framework of Eastonian political science and Parsonian social science. These earlier schemes simply cannot supply the answer to the core question: Why are German Nazism and Italian Fascism different? They could only infer a mechanical correlation between economic system and ideological beliefs. But once social research moves beyond a fourfold organizational table, or a nine-part stratification chart, and makes critical decisions about human behavior, we are forced to examine the cultural foundations of decisionmaking; doing so compels us to reconsider ethnicity, nationality, and religiosity.

Imagine yourself to be a Jew fleeing from Eastern Europe; and further envision that you are trapped in Basel, Switzerland, during World War II. You cannot stay in Switzerland because the Swiss do not want new immigrants or citizen participation. However, being generous of nature, they will supply you with a one-way ticket to Berlin, Rome, or Moscow—your choice. If you are a pure Parsonian or a pure Eastonian, you are not easily able to decide. But if you are a normal person, perhaps with a family to care for and contend with, and have to leave Basel quickly, you know exactly where you have to go. The rational, i.e., survival, attitude of course dictates going to Rome.

Such personal, even intimate decisions embody the essence of political anthropology. It is exactly what the question of religion and state, or religion and politics must cope with at higher levels of generality. Culture is the combination of informal, human forces that determine actual political behavior in specific circumstances. Building a political anthropology does not require a construction of an abstract theorem but deciding upon concrete actions based on cultural norms. Political anthropology also spares us from moving to another level of systems building and systems maintenance to replace older paradigms that do not work. Field researchers have to take into account the relationship of human forces, so that the very notion of system itself becomes infused by a consideration of cultural phenomena. Once this is done, we are practicing political anthropology of a relatively high order: (1) we look carefully at real events; (2) we think in terms of categories of a much more interpersonal range without using an inherited model-building infrastructure; and (3) we develop analytic frameworks that make no presumption of metaphysical dualism.

If this makes sense, then developments within the Third World, and even within the Second, Soviet World, also begin to make sense. The dualism, the separation of science from religion, the enlightenment vision of the world that social researchers remain children of, or better hostage to, does not obtain for most of humanity. It does not obtain for the Polish working class; it does not obtain for the Iranian masses; it does not obtain for Israelis who have a sense of destiny bound with culture; it does not obtain for Palestinians in search of national identity; it does not obtain with African organizations, which we call tribal but which more often link religiosity, tribe, nation, state in a new more complex hegemonic relationship.

The dualism between state and religion, no less than science and religion, that we have inherited fails us when we try to understand real events, because they occur as a rebellion against modernity as such. Scholars do not rebel against David Easton or Talcott Parsons but against a concept of modernity implied by their kind of systematic, structural, Westernized model of the world. For better or worse, we live in a world of rebellion against the dualism that we have often taken to be normative in character. Once they are no longer seen as normative, once they are seen as operational in monistic (or pluralistic) no less than dualistic terms, then events in Eastern Europe or the Middle East begin to make sense.

Political upheaval in a nation like Poland could scarcely take on a meaningful or massive form other than as a Roman Catholic Church formation. How could a breakdown of ideology within the rigid framework made possible by the Soviet orbit be dealt with outside a theological restoration? Similarly, in Iran, what options to the modernizing system that the Persian shah imposed upon the nation, other than the Shiite form of Muslim belief, are feasible in mass organizational terms? This is not to make judgments about this mullah versus that shah; rather it is to observe that the terms of political discourse, the terms of policymaking in many nations and regions, are saturated with religiosity—not as an abstract framework concerning the nature of God's will but, rather, as the values that ought to bind people in terms of modernization, developmentalism, and industrialism.

If a political anthropology is perceived in global terms, the contemporary world, particularly the developing areas, makes more sense. When culture once again is introduced as a critical variable in the analysis of state power and religious rationalization, political anthropology becomes a new paradigm, itself a synthetic view of the political structure. That is why the work being done within the anthropological and political groups studying religion and state power is so important. Feudalism sought to spiritualize the material basis of production. Capitalism sought to make a spiritual impulse out of material culture. Whatever the merits of these efforts, we have now achieved and appreciate that the dualism of politics and religion may not be a cosmic certainty after all—but simply two varieties of the same human theme of life and death: the survival and termination of systems no less than people, organizations no less than organisms.

Note

Remarks presented as chair and discussant of the panel "Religion and State Building" at the 78th annual meeting of the American Political Science Association, Denver, September 2-5, 1982.

2

The Bible in the American Political Tradition

Wilson Carey McWilliams

The Bible is the great gate to Western culture, an indispensable key to our language, meanings, and thought.[1] Scripture, moreover, has a special importance in American political thought and history. The Bible, I will be arguing, has been the second voice in the grand dialogue of American political culture, an alternative to the "liberal tradition" set in the deepest foundations of American life.[2]

I will also be contending, consequently, that increasing unfamiliarity with the Bible makes it harder and harder for Americans to understand their origins and their mores, or to put words to their experiences. More and more, Americans speak a language shaped by liberalism and by the more extreme individualisms that are liberalism's contemporary heirs.[3] Lacking knowledge of the Bible, Americans are likely to be literally inarticulate, unable to relate themselves to American life and culture as a whole and locked a little more securely in Tocqueville's prison of the self.[4]

In the first place, my concern here is with the Bible, not religion. People who are not religious in any orthodox sense may revere or be deeply influenced by the Bible; in American thought, Melville is an obvious example.[5] At the same time, there are numberless people who are deeply religious but who have only a limited or superficial knowledge of the Bible and its doctrines. It is also worth remembering, especially in contemporary America, that there is no shortage of nonbiblical, or even antibiblical, religions.[6]

Before turning to America, I will try to spell out the main lines of the Bible's teaching about politics. Like Dumezil, I will be speaking of the "structures of thought" rather than the "reconstitution of events."[7] Consequently, I will make only passing references to the history *of* the Bible or to the Bible *as* history.[8] My purpose here is with a text and a doctrine, and as with all didactics, the way in which the Bible teaches is inseparable from what is taught.

At the outset, it is important to distinguish sacred writing from other forms of religious communication. In Revelation, God addresses specific persons. His presence is felt with overwhelming force and verifies itself, at least for the moment, although lapses and doubts may set in later on.[9] Preaching also speaks to specific audiences and is likely to be tailored to the immediate needs and concerns of the hearers. Scripture, however, is "proclaimed to the whole world," or at least to all literate persons. Its audience is radically unspecific. The Bible can be read by base and evil people; at the same time, it speaks of high and extraordinary things, beyond the reach of custom and law. Scripture is patently dangerous: Charles Manson, to take only one recent example, found a warrant for mass murder in Revelation.

Yet the risk of Scripture is linked to its egalitarian character. Preaching makes the teacher the focus of attention and authority; it relies on the teacher's eloquence and cannot be separated from the impact of his or her person. This is especially true because preachings ordinarily cannot be reexamined. Audiences listen more or less passively, and they hear the preacher's message from the outside. The Puritan congregation of Hawthorne's *Scarlet Letter* mistook Arthur Dimmesdale's spiritual anguish for a kind of holiness, and its reverence only made matters worse. Preaching, consequently, has to be judged on the same principle that makes Jesus's words preferable to his works: We owe greater respect to whatever takes us closer to the heart of things.[10]

Scripture, in contrast to preaching, is relatively impersonal. It persuades by words and images, arguments and testimonies. It can also be put to the question repeatedly. Moreover, the reader is a far more active participant than the hearer. Scripture is silent. Consequently, even if I sincerely intend to be guided by the author, I can never be certain that my reading corresponds to the author's meaning. This blurs the line between the author and the reader: I cannot be certain what is the author's and what is mine. Scripture thus reduces the ambivalence of the taught, the human resistance to being instructed offered in the name of dignity.   Israel, the Bible tells us, is "stiff-necked" because the people resist being "fed."[12] Moses must "make an end of speaking" before Israel can really be asked to "set your hearts on all the words which I testify."[13]

The Bible is democratic in another sense. It is a single text and can be common ground for a people. Differences in understanding arise from differences in the depth of one's reading without losing that dimension of commonality. Hence, patterning themselves on the Scripture, the Puritans sought a "plain style" that could speak to the "common auditory" and "direct the apprehensions of the meanest."[14]

Nevertheless, the Bible does teach different things to different levels of understanding. Moses tells parents that they must *command* their children to follow the law as the "life" of the people.[15] But a parent cannot order a child to set his or her "heart" on the law. Parents can only demand that the child observe and study the law, hoping that through practice and reading the child will learn what cannot be commanded.[16]

Similarly, Paul wrote, "From a child thou hast known the holy scriptures which are able to make thee wise unto salvation through faith in Christ Jesus." Paul's comment presumes that there is a distinction between knowing the Scriptures with a child's mastery and being made wise by Scripture. Paul also follows tradition in regarding wisdom as the highest reward of Scripture.[17] Salvation is not the distinctive gift of the Bible, because God can and does save souls without scriptural learning. Yet Scripture must convey its wisdom in the same words with which it teaches fools.

The more seriously one takes Scripture, the more one is compelled to assume that the words, order, and relationship of biblical texts reflect that complex educational task. The Bible includes folk stories and familiar songs, and it is full of borrowings. All of these elements, however, have been edited for a purpose.[18] In fact, Lévi-Strauss (following Wellhausen) regards Scripture as "deformed" because its editors made it intellective, without the "spontaneous" quality of folk culture.[19] That criticism, of course, only emphasizes the design of Scripture. "This is not mere compilation," Martin Buber wrote, "but a composition of the greatest kind."[20]

Conflicts and ambiguities in the text were permitted to remain there, which raises the possibility that they are intended. The Bible, for example, contains two accounts of the death of Saul. According to the first, Saul fell on his own sword when no one in his entourage would slay him; in the second story, Saul was slain by an Amalekite who seems to have had some vague connection to David's court. The Bible places these stories in adjoining chapters but in different books. A sporadic reader might miss the discrepancy, but any serious student is bound to notice it.[21] The text, in other words, leaves its attentive readers with a mystery. Complexities and incoherences of this sort pose questions and invite—even *drive*—reflective readers to seek answers to their riddles.[22]

Similarly, Scripture is allusive, and allusion suggests comparison to the material to which it refers. Only those who recognize the allusion, of course, can begin to think about its meaning. Cross-references and concordances are helpful, but allusion is often subtler than such mechanical devices comprehend. Calum Carmichael points out, for example, that Deuteronomy is a farewell speech of Moses to Israel, modeled on the farewell speech of Jacob to his sons. As such, it encourages reflection on the relation between the new, Deuteronomy's explicit law, and the old, the order of custom and clan right. It calls attention, in other words, to the distinction between tribal and political society, to the different mode of speech appropriate to each, and to the change from the Assembly of Israel to the Assembly of the Lord.[23]

"The ancient classics and Bibles," Thoreau wrote, are ordinarily read "as the multitude read the stars, astrologically, not astronomically." Thoreau's prescription for reading such scriptures is to the point: "We must laboriously seek the meaning of each word and line, conjecturing a larger sense than common use permits out of what wisdom and valor and generosity we have."[24] This approach to the Bible is, in any case, especially important in the American context because the most biblical of classical American writers (Melville and Hawthorne, for example) took a similar position.[25]

Any higher understanding of Scripture, however, must grow out of reflection on the text as commonly understood. Allegorical interpretations, for instance, ought to be distrusted because they tell us to ignore or slight the apparent meaning.[26] At the highest level, the Song of Solomon may refer to the relation between God and His people or between Christ and the church. The Song speaks, however, about love in the ordinary, fleshly sense. Any exalted meaning, then, must derive from the proposition that profane love points toward sacred love. In these terms, learning about incarnate love and its limitations—being wise about love—is a step, possibly an essential one, to knowledge of higher love.[27]

So understood, Scripture can help to answer a democratic mystery. Democracy grows out of the claim of the many to share in the highest things, a leveling up that aims to raise all citizens to the highest possible human stature. This democratic aspiration, however, is at odds with democratic practice. Democratic politics gives commonplace human beings the authority to decide the highest questions of human and political life. Inevitably, democratic practice tends to associate the *norm* with the *average*, leveling down where democratic aspiration raises up. For much of American history, I will argue, the Bible provided the common term between equality and excellence in American political life. If this is true, the declining biblicality of American culture debases our political life.[28] That conclusion is doubly alarming because our times may prove to demand great sacrifice and, hence, a democratic kind of political nobility. That high excellence is a central goal of the Bible's teaching; in the biblical view, all human things are subject to sacrifice.

Biblical religion proclaims that God made man in His own image, but human beings can frame no likeness of God. Nothing in the created world is worthy of worship; no earthly institution is sacred; all this-worldly devotion must be qualified and conditional.[29] The Bible is thus at odds with myth, for myths support and justify the existing patterns and perceptions—the "being and structure"—of society.[30] Myths justify established orders; the Bible demands that established orders justify themselves. As this suggests, biblical religion is never civil religion: It claims the right to judge cities, and it asks that the city serve what is divine.[31]

Like all human societies, ancient Israel developed mythic justifications for its institutions. These lesser and greater idolatries, however, never became as deeply rooted and stable as the mythologies of other nations. The Bible demanded and legitimated a critical stance toward the polity and its life, most visibly reflected in the repeated prophetic assaults on the complacencies of custom, material power, and law.[32]

Nevertheless, Frankfort and his associates exaggerate when they assert that in ancient Hebrew thought "man and nature are necessarily *valueless* before God."[33] Idolatry is disproportionate in placing the creature at the center of creation, but a just correction requires acknowledgment of the creature's real worth. All created things have a value derived from creation and its Author: "And God saw everything that He had made, and behold, it was very good."[34] This goodness, however, pertains to human beings (and to all created things) only as parts of the whole.[35]

The Bible confronts us with the fact that human things are vulnerable, contingent, and doomed to oblivion:

> As for man, his days are as grass.
> As a flower of the field, so he flourisheth.
> For the wind passeth over it, and it is gone;
> And the place thereof shall know it no more.[36]

Human achievements and excellences are transient and imperfect.[37] But this desolating reminder of human partiality is intended to help in enlisting human allegiance for the whole, the Word that endures.[38] Similarly, the Bible seeks to free human beings from idolatrous polities and societies in order to establish political regimes that, recognizing their own partiality, are more truly just. Politics, like humankind, needs to be born again.[39]

The Bible's teaching about politics begins with the story of Cain and Abel. According to that story, God has "respect" for Abel's offering of the firstlings of his flock but not for Cain's fruit. God's preference is not explained, and this silence is willful: The Bible pointedly does *not* assert that Abel was preferred because the pastoral life is better than that of agriculture, although that notion was common folklore. The Bible confronts us with an act that seems arbitrary, like such manifestations of divine favor as beauty or good birth. God surely has a reason for favoring Abel, but that reason is not apparent. The story is not concerned with God's reasons but with Cain's reactions.

Cain regards God's "respect" as a private benefice, not as a common benefit. Hence, Abel's receipt of God's respect reflects on Cain's dignity. Yet the family as a group is blessed by Abel's good fortune. Similarly, to the extent that my brother is "mine," his successes are also mine and enhance, rather than detract from, my dignity. Cain's sense of commonality, however, is too weak to outweigh his private resentments. To that extent, it matters that Cain is a farmer and Abel is a shepherd. Whatever the respective merits of these forms of work, the fact that they are different shows a family beginning to specialize, losing the common work, way of life, and fortune that are the material basis of simple community.[40] But specialization does not excuse Cain; it *tempts* him to be blind to the less palpable aspects of community, but such temptations, God tells Cain, can and must be mastered.[41] Cain's spirit, however, does not govern; it submits to and rationalizes the demand for private dignity that is rooted in the body and its senses.

Cain's later reaction to his punishment shows, in fact, how individualistic he really is. God makes Cain a "fugitive and a wanderer," and Cain, in response, gives three reasons that his punishment is unbearable: (1) God will hide his face from Cain, (2) Cain will be a fugitive and a stranger, and (3) he will be subject to be slain by whoever finds him. God protects Cain against only the last of these dangers, but that evidently makes the sentence bearable. Cain cannot endure the threat of violent death, but he finds it supportable to be alienated from God and man.[42] Cain is destined to a life among strangers, all more or less hostile, who stop short of killing him. It is, consequently, appropriate for Cain to found a city, since that condition describes urban life, at least in its corrupt form.[43]

There is an undeniable suspicion of the city in this story because the city is a human problem. The city, as compared with the village, accentuates the tendency of specialization to call community into question. Social, economic, and emotional distance increases and the sense of the city as a whole is lost.[44] Commercial life, moreover, means that the need of one person is another's chance for gain, and money economies remove the limits to avarice.[45] It was common in the ancient Middle East to see a city disintegrate into estranged interests and expel or crowd out debtors or losing political factions.[46] Any city founded by Cainlike individualists is doomed to decay.

Because a city of individualists lacks internal unity, it can acquire the *appearance* of unity only through external goals, the desire to defeat enemies or to gain wealth. But if the common enemy is defeated, he is no longer a reason for unity, and wealth, once acquired, becomes only so many private possessions. The individualistic city, consequently, must seek out new and ever-greater projects—it depends on "growth," as we say today. Hence Babel's reason for building its tower to heaven: "lest we be scattered upon the face of the whole earth."[47] Because such cities are compelled to attempt more and more ambitious projects, however, they will inevitably attempt the impossible. When that occurs, it is not really necessary for God to confuse a city's speech; the citizens of Babel never really spoke the same language.

Yet that story, with all its contemporary echoes, suggests another kind of city, one that would cultivate common speech and internal justice, eschewing expansion and the quest for mastery.[48] In Deuteronomy, the term "city" refers to the city seen from the outside, the city as defined by its externalities and appearances. A city so self-defined would necessarily be hollow. By contrast, the term "gates" refers to the city seen from within or in its inward life, especially in the dispensing of justice.[49] Hence the peculiar appropriateness of the spiritual "Twelve Gates to the City." A polis is unjust and corrupt, in the biblical view, unless it sees its gates as avenues leading in, not superhighways leading out. A city's gates, in this sense, are the mark of its political covenant.[50]

Law and ritual may be the signs of a covenant, but they do not create it. A covenant is based on a perceived likeness of spirit, a common idea of justice, and a deeply felt sense of being one despite the differences of private interest. The good city depends on the psychological willingness and ability to covenant. The heart of political wisdom, then, is knowledge about the spiritual pilgrimage that prepares and educates the soul.

The political education of the soul is a task of intimidating difficulty. Idolatry of self is the most pervasive and ineradicable of all idolatries. Original Sin involves the effort to make the self the center of creation or, failing that, to enable the self to be separate and independent. In either case, the effect is to deny one's human status as part of the whole.[51]

The manifestation of self-idolatry is a desire to control and enhance "my own," my body and the things connected to it, most notably my family (and especially, the "heirs of my body") and my property.[52] All human beings follow these impulses to some degree. Yet implicitly, the desire to preserve and advance my own implies a rejection of all limits on my will, the most remarkable being my mortality. Self-idolatry entails a struggle to master nature.

This, Scripture teaches, is an unhappy condition, haunted by anxieties, because it is based on illusions and a flight from humanity's true nature. Paradoxically, self-centeredness is really self-denial.[53] Human beings need to be brought to justice—to the recognition that they are dependent parts of a good whole—in order to be reconciled to themselves. It is not enough for law and nature to restrain us; we need to perceive God's creation as a good in order to value our own finite status.[54]

God teaches this lesson to His chosen by a combination of desolation and mercy.[55] Abraham, surrounded by the carcasses of sacrificed animals, feels a "horror of great darkness"; Jacob is forced to humble himself before Esau and loses his son Joseph; Joseph is cast into a pit and sold into exile. Devastating experience shatters the defenses of the self, leaving the individual—for the moment at least—with an overwhelming sense of finitude. But Abraham is then promised that his line will be a great nation, and he is given a son in his old age; Esau welcomes Jacob generously, and Israel lives to be reunited with Joseph; Joseph becomes first in Egypt after Pharaoh and recovers his family. These are extraordinary blessings that most human beings will not share. Nevertheless, they afford their recipients a glimpse of God's design, a conviction that the whole is lovely as well as irresistible: "You meant evil against me, but God meant it for good. . . ."[56]

Abraham and his descendants gradually develop a sense of participation in wider social and political wholes. Beginning as a family, narrowly distrustful of the world around it and able to adjust internal conflicts only by dissolving into separate patriarchal households, Israel becomes first a tribal society and then a people. After the fall of the false city, Babel, God leads Israel to a new sort of political knowledge.[57]

God's instruction of Israel furnishes a model for political society, for a rightly constructed polity aims to produce public-spirited citizens who also accept their place within God's order. Political society needs to limit and constrain its citizens, demanding sacrifice and punishing them when needed. In so doing, it imitates—in a small, relatively ineffective way—God's desolation of pride. At the same time, a good political order nurtures, educates, and improves its citizens: Its chastenings are intended to help teach the lesson that the whole is a good order. The duty to care for the poor is an example of both constraint and nurturance. Good citizens are openhearted to their fellows, but those who will not be openhearted can, and should, be compelled to be openhanded.[58] Covetousness is the only *feeling* forbidden by the Decalogue, because community is wounded by envy and avarice alike.[59] The liberal heresy that denies the need for constraint and punishment abandons the means; conservative acceptance of hardheartedness rejects the end.

In no way does Scripture teach that "moral men" are involved in "immoral society."[60] Reinhold Niebuhr's argument, that individuals have moral faculties and political societies do not, is founded in the liberal, individualistic notion that societies and polities are artificial, existing by convention only. The Bible regards peoples as wholes, not merely as collections of individuals, and hence publics are rightly judged as collectivities.

Abraham's argument against God at Sodom—that it is unjust to destroy the righteous with the wicked—seems to point to the conclusion that God cannot rightfully destroy Sodom if there is even one just person in the city. The Lord breaks off the argument but the question remains: Because Lot is a decent man, how can God rightly destroy Sodom? In fact, Abraham's case is defective because Abraham speaks of righteousness solely in relation to individuals. Lot does not actively participate in Sodom's evil, but he lives in the city and shares its fortunes. He intended to marry his daughters to Sodomites; even when warned of the city's doom, he lingers and has to be seized and led out. Dependent on the city, Lot cannot live without urban life. He is a part of the whole, and despite his private virtues he bears a share of the city's guilt. God spares Lot out of mercy, not justice.[61]

Nevertheless, the Bible teaches that public spirit will always be opposed by private interest. Education out of self-idolatry is always imperfect. The body continues to make claims against the spirit. Bonds based on righteousness, covenants among the kindred of spirit, must compete with blood kinship, property, and pride. Abraham, called out of his father's house, has been taught repeatedly that blood kinship is less important than righteousness. Yet at the end of his life, Abraham sends his servant to seek a wife for Isaac in Abraham's old country from among Abraham's blood kin. The servant, with a better sense of priorities, chooses Rebekah because she is hospitable to servants and even to animals. Wiser in the ways of human dependence, the servant knows that a generous spirit is more important than bloodline.[62] Yet the servant does not choose Rebekah because he believes her to be the best possible wife for Isaac; he selects her because she is the best within the terms set by Abraham. Servants—public or private—must recognize that the spirit is compelled to make concessions to the limitations of the flesh.

Similarly, Joseph rises out of slavery because he understands the mutability of political favor and fortune and, hence, can profit from the false optimism of others.[63] Yet Joseph brings his people into Egypt and gives them a privileged and resented position in a regime that depends on the life and favor of one man. Joseph's pride in his own statecraft and the regime it has created overrides his more fundamental wisdom. Elevated by Joseph, all Israel is cast into slavery, a collective desolation, and subsequently receives from God the blessing of liberation. The instruction of this shared experience transforms the children of Israel into a people.[64] Even on this grand scale, however, political education is imperfect. Israel's collective wisdom, even more than that of its founders, is sporadic and uncertain.

Given human shortcomings, even the best political regime is twice limited. In the first place, a political society cannot rely simply on the virtue of its people. A covenant polity requires a unity of spirit, but it also depends on law and institutions to protect the political society when human beings forget or fail. The second constraint is only a little less obvious. The larger the political society, the greater the tension between body and spirit, private feelings and public duties. The increased resistance of the body means, in turn, that large states must rely more on force or appeals to private interest and less on patriotism and public spirit. Political order is likely to be little more than external conformity. In a large state, covenants are fragile if they exist at all; megalopolis, like the idols, rests on feet of clay. The body's parochiality, consequently, imposes a limitation on the size of good political regimes. A world regime, logically indicated by the common nature of humankind, is not suited to fallen humanity. The politics of covenant presumes a world of cities and nations.[65]

Even the best political society, however, is only part of the whole. The nations are subject to the Kingdom of God, and all are liable to sacrifice and judgment.[66] Even chosen Israel is only a part—though a uniquely important one—of the order of things. All regimes can become idols, and Israel's often does; only the fortunate have true prophets to attempt to set them right.[67] In fact, false prophets are moved, more often than not, by a kind of patriotism, perverting "the conditional promise to an Israel that would accomplish its tasks into an unconditional security for all time."[68]

Jonah sought to evade God's call to prophesy in Nineveh because he foresaw that Nineveh would repent and be forgiven.[69] Jonah presumably wanted Nineveh, Israel's ancient enemy, to be destroyed. Moreover, Jonah's pride was involved: Because he had prophesied doom, God's clemency made him look the fool. Nineveh's repentance, however, improves God's creation because the whole is benefited by the excellence of its parts.[70] Pride of state and pride of word must yield, consequently, to the hope that all human beings, becoming more just, may be reconciled to each other and to God.

Let me summarize the Bible's teaching about politics as I have presented it here. (1) Human beings are not born "free and independent." They are subject to limits and are assigned a place in the order of creation; they depend on God, on their fellow humans, and on nature. (2) Human beings begin with a desire for independence and a yearning to do as they will, but this is the result of sin, not the true nature of humanity. (3) Society and polity exist to educate human beings out of self-concern to the greatest extent possible. (4) The good political society is founded on a covenant, a spiritual and moral union, and cultivates justice and fraternity rather than material power, preferring inner excellence to external expansion. (5) Such a regime, given human frailties, must be limited in size and governed by law. (6) The polity is itself a part of the whole, limited and ruled by a higher law. There are, of course, other interpretations of Scripture. These propositions are at least a reasonable approximation of the biblical view as Americans originally understood it, and they provide a foundation for examining the place of the Bible in American political thought.

Biblical doctrine played a special role in the founding of America. The Bible was the only common text for white America; it soon became almost the only positive bond between blacks and whites. If biblicism was a Protestant predisposition, the Bible was not. Scripture was a common point of reference for groups with differing and often hostile pasts, and a stable beacon for peoples who had broken their ties to custom. In the absence of established institutions, the Bible often served as a law-book, one far more popular than the already "mysterious," lawyerly science of common law.[71]

The most familiar appeal to Scripture, of course, is the Puritan effort to found a Bible polity based on covenant, a concern for fraternity rather than "great things," and the hope of subjecting commerce to moral and legal regulation.[72] Puritan teachings have been studied too often and too well to need exposition here.[73] It does matter, however, that Puritan doctrines, though more intellectual and probably more coherent than comparable teachings, were part of a broadly similar body of teaching pervading colonial America.

Yet despite the centrality of the Bible in early American culture, the founding generation rejected or deemphasized the Bible and biblical rhetoric. It was, as Alan Heimert comments, a kind of interlude in which gentlemanly conventions and Roman cadences dominated public speech.[74] There were exceptions, like Patrick Henry, but the rule was clear. The Bible, moreover, was even less evident in the Framers' political thought.

Against this thesis, Bellah and Hammond contend that the Creator of the Declaration of Independence is a "distinctly biblical God . . . who creates individual human beings and endows them with equality and fundamental rights."[75] This argument, however, is wrong on two counts. In the first place, it misstates the Declaration: Human beings are "created equal," not endowed with equality. They are endowed with equal *rights*, a rather different idea.[76] Second, while the "biblical God" undeniably creates human beings, it is far from clear that He endows them with individual rights. The Declaration's language is designed to be acceptable to deists and orthodox believers alike, but this prudential ambiguity is not enough to make the Creator of the Declaration, "Nature's God," the "distinctly biblical God" who is beyond nature and Lord over it.

Even the Declaration's equivocal religiosity is absent from the Constitution and the theory on which it is based. There is no reference to the Bible, as far as I know, in all of *The Federalist*. Madison does refer to divine beings in *The Federalist* 51, but his rhetorical allusion itself indicates the difference between Madison's view and the Bible's teaching. Madison asserts that men and angels differ politically because angels need no government. In the Bible, of course, angels are not only governed, they are capable of rebellion.[77] And the most famous biblical reference to men and angels, 1 Corinthians 13:1, suggests that men and angels, in one decisive respect, are comparable in speech, the most political of all faculties: "If I speak with the tongues of men and of angels, and have not charity, I am become as a sounding brass or a tinkling crystal." In the biblical view, politicality is characteristic of both the human and the divine; for Madison, politics—"the greatest of all reflections on human nature"—is unworthy of the divine.

The Framers' doctrine speaks of the rights of individuals who are free in the state of nature, rather than referring to their duties within the order of nature. In the political science of the Framers, political society is a convenience meant to serve private rights. Politics is intended to protect liberty, the "diversity in the faculties of men," rather than regulating that diversity for the good of the public as a whole. In the strict sense, there is no public and no whole: There are only individual rights, on one hand, and "permanent and aggregate interest" on the other. In this new science of politics, institutions and an extensive republic are to substitute for the covenant as a means of controlling factions.[78] Moreover, human beings—in the Framers' teaching—are at war with nature, seeking the mastery that will force nature to yield to their desires. The political regime, their creature, is consequently dedicated to the pursuit of power, which is another argument for a large, commercial republic. In all these respects, the Framers' theories are at odds with the Bible's teaching.[79]

The Framers recognized that opposition and even welcomed it because they associated the political claims of religion with persecution and with the murderous strife of religious war. Accordingly, the Framers were concerned to make religion harmless, rendering it safely subject to political society without even the hope of rule. Madison regarded freedom of religion as an absolute right because he considered religion to be radically private and subjective. It is not much more difficult, Madison wrote Jefferson, to devise a religious creed than to frame a political one, but the public has some claim to do the second and none to do the first.[80] Religion lacks any objective, public, or rational foundation; it belongs wholly to the world of "opinions."

In the Framers' design, religion is presumably limited, like other "factions," because—according to the familiar argument of *The Federalist* 10, a multitude of sects will be unable to "concert and execute their plans of oppression." In the case of religion, however, Madison was not content to leave it at that: The original Constitution rules out any form of religious test, and Madison shaped the language of the First Amendment to rule out religious establishment at the federal level. (Madison held identical views about the place of religion in the states.)[81] As this indicates, Madison regarded religion as uniquely dangerous, less rational than other factions, less subject to the moderating effects of interest, and more capable of mobilizing majority opinion on its behalf.

Paine's *Common Sense* is almost alone among the great works of the founders in making an explicit appeal to the Bible. Clearly, however, Paine invoked Scripture because he aimed to reach a wider public that revered the Bible and knew virtually no other book.[82] Paine's own view that the Bible is "absurd" and a "book of fables" was not openly expressed until much later, in *The Age of Reason*. Yet Paine's rejection of the Bible is only a little less evident in *Common Sense*.

Paine begins his comments on Scripture with the assertion that ''the quiet and rural lives of the first patriarchs'' have a ''happy something'' lacking in the history of Jewish monarchy. This is an outrageous statement on its face: The lives of the patriarchs are anything but quiet. Moreover, Paine is purposefully vague about the ''happy something'' that the patriarchal world allegedly possessed.[83]

He goes on to make the correct observation that Israel copied kingship from the heathen, and he offers two examples of the godlessness of monarchy. The first (Judges 8:22-23) cites Gideon's rejection of a crown in favor of rule by the Lord. But immediately after declaring that ''the Lord shall rule over you,'' Gideon asks for gold loot, which he makes into an ephod,'' ''and all Israel went thither a whoring after it, which thing became a great snare to Gideon and to his house'' (Judges 8:27). Because a golden ephod was a high priest's vestment, Gideon seems to have assumed a self-consecrated high priesthood.[84] Did Gideon proclaim the Lord's rule only to claim the right to speak for Lord as a sort of covert king concealed by a mantle of divine authority? There is good evidence for such an interpretation: The name of Gideon's son, Abimelech, means ''my father is king.''[85]

Like Gideon, Paine wraps himself in a divine disguise. Later in *Common Sense*, Paine imitates Gideon by declaring that the king of America ''reigns above.'' For secular purposes, Paine goes on, Americans ought to place their constitution on the ''divine law, the word of God.'' Then, crowning the constitution, they should proclaim that ''the law is king.'' The rule of law, consequently, rests on divine foundations and seems to derive its authority from God's higher law. Paine goes on to argue, however, that the law's crown ought to be broken up and ''scattered among the people, whose right it is.''[86] The real sovereign is not the king above but the people below. Moroever, if the people have the right to rule over secular law, but secular law rests on divine law, popular sovereignty entails the right to rule over divine law as well.

Paine's second example from Scripture seems more straightforward because he cites Samuel's enumeration of the dangers of monarchy (1 Samuel 8:5-20). But Paine stops with verse 20; he omits Samuel's report to the Lord and the Lord's command, ''hearken unto their voice and make them a king'' (8:22). In fact, Paine then skips to 1 Samuel 12:17-19, although he conceals the omission (''Samuel continued to reason with them . . . and seeing them bent on their folly, he cried out. . . .''). Paine ends by announcing that ''these portions of Scripture'' demonstrate God's opposition to monarchical government. Consequently, Paine argues, there was ''as much of kingcraft as priestcraft in withholding the scripture from the people in popish countries.''[87] This appeal to Protestant prejudice takes on special significance because *Paine* has just withheld several portions of Scripture. In the omitted passages, God has chosen Saul to be king (1 Samuel 9:17) and Samuel has anointed him. Moreover, before Samuel's protest against kingship, cited by Paine

(12:17), Samuel has remarked that the Lord will punish His people, as He did their kingless ancestors, only if they do not follow His commandments and obey His voice. It is explicitly possible (although it may be unlikely), to combine kingly government and obedience to God (12:14). God does not favor kingship, and monarchy is not the best regime—in that, Paine is true to the text—but He does regard it as a legitimate form of rule.

A bit later, Paine refers to Saul as chosen "by lot"; Scripture claims that he was chosen by God. Paine is asserting that, in reality, God's providences and interventions, as claimed by Scripture, are chance occurrences when they are not "priestcraft." This argument comes closer to Paine's real aim. Paine contends that "original sin and hereditary succession are parallels." Does that imply that republican rule can overthrow *both*? So it seems, because Paine explicitly claims that America has the power to begin the world again.[88] In fact, Paine sees a clear parallel between overcoming British monarchy and overthrowing God's authority. Arguing against any reconciliation with Britain, Paine cites an idea that Milton "wisely expresses" (Paine is too honest to attribute the notion to Milton himself), "Never can true reconcilement grow where wounds of deadly hate have pierced so deep." Paine is citing, approvingly, Satan's rejection of any reconciliation with God.[89] This was a familiar text with ministers who supported the American Revolution, but they used it in the orthodox sense. Nathaniel Whitaker, for example, used Satan as the epitome of the "carnal mind" in arguing that the Tories would never be reconciled to America.[90] Whitaker praises the love that can overcome the deepest hate; Paine rejects it. In Paine's view, in other words, the revolution offers the opportunity to reject Christian forgiveness and humility in favor of a truly national self-assertion (the "happy something" of patriarchal days?) and the human claim to mastery. *Novus Ordo Secolorum*, in these terms, implies that the birth of the American republic amounts to the end of the Christian era.[91]

Very few of the Framers went as far as Paine; almost all believed that "religion," vaguely defined, was valuable to civil society. This support for religion, however, did not amount to an endorsement of the Bible or its teachings. Washington invoked religion, for example, because "refined education" is insufficient to establish morality and respect for oaths. Religion, in this view, is reduced to mythology: It *supports* but does not *define* the moral and civil order.[92]

Jefferson accepted Washington's argument—he wondered, for example, whether an atheist's testimony was reliable enough to be accepted at law—but he also went beyond it. Religion, in Jefferson's view, is needed to correct the narrow calculations of self-interest. Slavery is contrary to natural right, and ending slavery is in the interest of humanity as a whole because it removes a temptation to arrogance and a danger to liberty. But the abolition of slavery is not clearly in the interest of *slaveholders*; indeed, it seems likely that it is not. Because religion helps give human beings a more extended sense of their duties to humanity, it is invaluable as an ally of the "Heart" in addressing problems like slavery.[93] But Jefferson's diety speaks the language of natural right, not that of the Bible.

In what he meant to be a private letter, Jefferson made his own view explicit. He found the Hebrew Scriptures "degrading and injurious" in their ideas of God, and their ethics "not only imperfect, but often irreconcilable with the sound dictates of reason and morality." He revered Jesus. Nevertheless, Jefferson found the New Testament's account of Jesus's teachings to be "mutilated, misstated and often unintelligible," doubtless because Jesus's life was recorded by "unlettered and ignorant men" relying on their memories after a lapse of years. Even with all these apologies, he considered Jesus's doctrine to be "defective as a whole." It is hardly surprising, then, that Jefferson thought that the Bible should not be put into the hands of children until their minds had been shaped for "religious inquiries" by other sources.[94]

Jefferson was among the most religious of the Framers, and his views were broadly characteristic of the founders. The Bible, in this way of thinking, is sometimes wise and useful, but it is often false, fabulous, and perverse. It needs to be subordinated to the enlightened doctrine in which the first political principle is not God's Kingdom but human freedom.

For the moment, the Framers had their way. Yet as Gordon Wood observes, within a generation the American public—aided by a major increase in literacy and in publishing—intruded on and contended with the enlightened culture of the gentry.[95] The public brought with it a political culture heavily influenced by the Bible to rival the liberalism of the Framers. That evangelical Christians made common cause with leaders like Jefferson should not obscure their very different modes of thought.[96]

Fear for the dissenting churches led Isaac Backus to support the ban on religious establishment, but Backus explicitly rejected the idea of "natural right," correctly recognizing that it contradicted the Bible's teaching.[97] Although Backus opposed state aid to any *one* church, he denied that religion was a private matter. The public, Backus argued, has a legitimate interest in supporting religion through Sabbath laws, censorial legislation, and even required public worship.[98] Backus aimed at a distinctly Christian state, one very similar to the "Christian Sparta" for which Sam Adams hoped.[99]

Because the Bible was the high culture of the many, it should not be surprising that even very radical democrats often strove for some form of religious test, such as a profession of faith or a declaration of belief in the Bible.[100] The central political idea of the "awakened," however, was not some form of religious establishment; it was the biblical idea of covenant, the conviction that a political society rests on a civic bond and a unity of spirit. Political institutions are important, but they are only the letter, empty forms that are given life and meaning by the spirit behind them. The Constitution and the laws, in this view, are only superficial indications of the nature of American political society. Public and private spheres intertwine; "the state" can never be separated from "society."[101]

Evangelical religion also maintained the biblical hostility to acquisitiveness and competitive ethics. This was not necessarily an ascetic view. In fact, the critics of "the emerging capitalist ethic" often observed that the limitless desire for riches is itself a form of asceticism. Rather, the critique of acquisitiveness emphasized the danger of self-seeking to the covenant and the threat of the "aristocratic spirit" to republican life.[102] Even a "Turk's paradise" of luxury, Gilbert Tennent declared, is a less serious temptaton and moral peril than the desire to be "a sort of independent Being."[103]

As Heimert notes, the liberal-rationalists among the clergy were torn between the traditional view that human beings are political and social by nature and the newer, more individualistic doctrine of natural right. Evangelical leaders, by contrast, were far more likely to defend the biblical teachings that true freedom is found in obedience to the law of nature and in public-spirited citizenship.[104] Yet after the American Revolution, the evangelical clergy largely withdrew from political life, abandoning the field in the critical years of the founding. Disenchantment with the secularity of American politics helped to bring about this retreat, as Heimert observes, but a good deal of the explanation lies within evangelical doctrine itself.[105]

In the first place, the evangelical emphasis on the *insufficiency* of political and social institutions could and did slide over into a denial of the *value* of institutions, virtually rejecting any role for political and social life in the education of the spirit. This was particularly likely because the evangelical method, the appeal to the "gracious affections" of individuals, ran counter to the common good and the idea of the covenant, which were so prominent in the content of the evangelical message. The evangelical movement, in other words, tilted—despite the intentions of its founder—in the direction of political quietism and a fixation on the private conscience.[106]

The argument against institutions carried over into the evangelical view of the Bible. Edwards observed that human beings will be blind to the beauties and truth of Scripture without inward affection; interpretation is no better than the spirit behind it.[107] This orthodox proposition, however, led the evangelicals to slight the Bible as a *teacher* of the spirit. The evangelical clergy took less care than their Puritan predecessors to be faithful to the text. Instead, they used Scripture as a "storehouse of metaphor" in the hope of reaching and rousing the spirits of their listeners. In doing so, they abandoned the public text in favor of private experience, and the quest for lively images and stories often resulted in the loss of context and depth.[108]

The appeal to the reborn heart and to the "gracious affections" also weakened the Bible's recognition of the limitations imposed by body on the spirit. This, in turn, led evangelical preachers to slight the necessary imperfections and boundaries of covenant and spiritual unity. The Bible envisages a world of nations; Paul denies that these distinctions matter "in Christ," but he does not ignore the reality of national differences in the secular world. Souls may unite but the flesh divides, and fleshly human beings need the support of those to whom they are close and to whom they matter.[109] The human needs for nurturance and dignity demand small states and societies, and with them, narrower allegiances never fully identical with our larger duties. By contrast, the Awakening sometimes promised or seemed to promise that it could set the spirit free from the body, attaining a more than biblical felicity. In doing so, it pledged more than it could deliver, understating the barriers to public spirit in America and contributing, consequently, to disillusionment with political life.

Disenchantment with achieving the millennium by transforming spirits encouraged many evangelicals to identify the approach of the Kingdom with the historical process. In this view, the advance of science and technology was the herald of a future "spiritual advance."[110] Hawthorne detested this doctrine, satirizing its later versions in "The Celestial Railroad," and his hostility was appropriate. The spiritualization of progress established a common ground with the liberal tradition and weakened religion's critique of modern, secular society.[111]

Nevertheless, evangelical religion at its best remembered the biblical teaching on the limitations of the spirit. It did not promise, consequently, an imminent end of private spirit and partiality. Yet this more biblical evangelism also preserved the idea of the covenant. Madison made individual liberty his first principle and sought, on the model of mechanics, to balance the parts. The wiser evangelists took the common good for their standard and urged, on the model of music, that the parts be harmonized to the whole.[112] In so doing, they helped preserve the old teaching for a new time.

In the nineteenth century, the relationship between democracy and the Bible was unmistakable. Religion and citizenship were intertwined popular "romances."[113] The quest for community was the great theme of revivalism, and it found a parallel in the Jacksonian ideal of the Union and the hope for a new covenant, "inward and spiritual," to vivify the formal unity of the laws.[114] The language and stories of the Bible were the most meaningful forms of public speech, pervading oratory and establishing many of the terms and limits of civic deliberation and political life.[115]

Mass democracy made the Bible uniquely valuable as a check on the psychological tyranny of the majority. Religion, as Tocqueville observed, taught a law and a right superior to the will of the majority. It provided a basis for defying the majority—Divine monarchy invoked against secular democracy—and it urged the public to limit itself.[116] Scripture, in fact, was an even more specific barrier to the tyranny of the majority, because the ancient strictures against syncretism emphasized a duty to resist fashion and opinion in the service of a truth that is more than one among many.[117]

There was another side to religion, of course. Too many of the churches were persuaded to moralize competitive individualism, material success, and historical progress, and to elide, if not deny, the limits to human mastery and perfectibility. America may even have strengthened the perennial temptation to reduce religion to mythology, turning the sacred to the service of the profane. Yet, as Peter Berger observes, the Bible was always some sort of obstacle to the "spiritual mobilization" of the church in support of liberal, commercial, and political society. The very existence of the text, with its all-too-different message, was a standing reminder of moral compromises and betrayals of the faith.[118]

Civil religion could be far more comfortable with churches that limited the authority of the Bible or abandoned it altogether, freeing religion—as Channing put it—from the "low views" of "darker ages."[119] This was most evident in Transcendentalism, which exaggerated the faults of the Awakening into a kind of caricature. The Scriptures, Emerson declared, "have no epical integrity; are fragmentary; are not shown in their order to the intellect." At best, the words of the Bible are forms that imprison the spirit. Transcendentalism preferred to appeal to intuition, the Word written on the heart. It accentuated the individualism of evangelical religion, jettisoning all public standards for the discipline of the spirit, and it relied in a millennialistic way on the course of history to produce moral order out of the chaos of individual impulse. Men suffer, Emerson wrote, "under evils whose end they cannot see," and need to be assured that the good is "that which really is being done."[120]

It was a teaching that revolted Hawthorne and Melville, those two great voices of the biblical tradition. Repeatedly, they taught that individualism and the faith in technology were founded on the illusory attempt to deny or escape from the dependence and the capacity for evil that were ineradicable parts of the human soul. Creeds like Emerson's allowed and encouraged Americans to moralize indifference and impoverished political life, and slighted the human need for the support of friends.[121]

In Melville's *Israel Potter*, Benjamin Franklin is portrayed as the epitome of individualistic rationalism and, hence, the true voice of the tradition of the Framers. It was an advised choice: Franklin was already enshrined as a secular saint of the American Enlightenment. Melville began his description of Franklin with apparent respect, likening him to Jacob, especially in the "unselfish devotion which we are bound to ascribe to him.'' Bound by piety, perhaps; the Bible, as Melville knew very well, depicts Jacob as a cunning competitor and a successful swindler. Melville went on to note the ''worldly wisdom and polished Italian tact'' under Franklin's air of ''Arcadian unaffectedness.'' His final description was devastating: Franklin is a ''Machiavelli in tents,'' a combination of ancient and modern duplicity and self-seeking. Melville grouped Franklin with Jacob and Hobbes, a trinity suggesting Jacob's temperamental egotism, Hobbes's scientific individualism, and Franklin's extraordinary ability to disguise both these qualities with moralistic cant.[122]

In the event, Franklin deceives and defrauds Israel Potter in any number of ways. In Melville's imagery, *Jacob* (Franklin) thus robs and defeats *Israel* (Potter), reversing the order of Scripture. The Bible uses the two names to refer to the qualities warring in Israel's soul, contrasting the competitive Jacob's bitterness toward nature with Israel's acceptance, and Jacob's concern for the things of the body with Israel's ''inner sight'' and attention to the spirit.[123] In the King James translation, Israel even dies before Jacob, but it is Israel who prevails.[124] American individualism, Melville was suggesting, had improved on Jacob's egotism because it had a talent for moralization, which Jacob lacked, donning—as Franklin had—the masks of benevolence and science when either suited his purpose. In modern America, as Melville saw it, moral self-deception was deceiving and overcoming the spirit.[125]

In American philosophy, Caleb Sprague Henry shared Melville's dark vision. In his essay on progress, published in 1861, Henry treated history as a conflict between *civilization*, and with it the ''faculty of adopting means to ends,'' and *Christianity and reason*, which were able to set worthy ends. By nature, civilization is intended to be subordinate to the moral faculties. Left to itself, civilization pursues trivial or base ends—the enhancement of technique and, implicity, the gratification of every desire. What modern theory regards as ''progress,'' Henry argued, is only the progressive development of civilization, to which modern thought has given the ascendancy. Civilization will not—its admirers aside—add a moral and spiritual dimension: It will *weaken* moral influences with the passing of time, accenting civilization's own irrationalities, its tendency to encourage fraud, the degrading of the poor, and the pursuit of luxury. Commerce and ''enlightened self love'' will restrain war, as liberal theory hopes, but they are insufficient to bring peace. The constraints of civilization on war are, consequently, certain to fail. Civilization is set on a disaster course and humanity with it; only the possibility that God will intervene offers any hope to His children.[126]

Henry's vision was, in many ways, a model prophecy, and his arguments seem chillingly realistic in the light of our experience.[127] His own contemporaries, however, discounted or ignored Henry's case. Americans had their doubts about liberal political theory and commercial civilization, but—in public, at least—the naysayers were a minority. In any case, the crisis of slavery and the Union shouldered aside, for a time, American anxieties about the direction of modern life.

The Bible, of course, was cited on both sides of the slavery controversy. Its authority was too great for either side to surrender its claim on Scripture. Nevertheless, the biblical case for slavery was decisively the weaker of the arguments. The stronger element of the proslavery case is found in New Testament citations adjuring slaves to obey their masters. But those urgings barely tolerate slavery; they do not make it right. Paul tells a slave not to mind being a servant, but he goes on to tell him to accept freedom if he can get it, for the real condition of those who are called by God is to be free of men.[128] Christians, if not all human beings, are free by nature; slavery is only one of many conditions that must be tolerated in a corrupt, less-than-natural world.

Defenders of slavery also appealed to the curse on Canaan, but that argument is simply ludicrous. It *is* Canaan who is doomed to be a "servant of servants," and however we interpret this passage, applying it to Africans is spectacularly bad geography. The real authority for arguments based on supposed racial "inferiorities" lay in science, not Scripture.[129]

The antislavery forces, by contrast, pointed to the fact that the God of the Decalogue identifies himself as a liberator, and they also observed that the fugitive slave law was directly contrary to Scripture.[130] Moreover, the spiritual freedom attributed to Christians also seems to make liberty a higher law.

The doctrine of natural right contributed at least as much to the argument against slavery. Nevertheless, when Theodore Parker, the Transcendentalist preacher, armed a fugitive slave, he gave him a sword for his body and a Bible for his soul.[131] There was an important truth in Parker's gesture. The doctrine of natural right implied that it was enough to restore a slave to his or her natural freedom. Even a Christian thinker like Theodore Dwight Weld was tempted by the argument that ending slavery would itself redeem America. Scripture, by contrast, argued that it is futile to free the body and neglect the soul. Emancipation calls for more than striking off shackles; it demands nurturance and education in social and political life. Moreover, as Charles Grandison Finney proclaimed, any emancipation was bound to be superficial without repentance and rebirth in white America.[132] A change in the laws is empty, mere form, unless it is preceded by or leads to a change in the covenant.

Lincoln recognized that the slavery issue pointed to a deeper spiritual crisis in the Union. His reference to the "house divided," for example, reaches beyond slavery to the nature of political freedom itself.[133] The most familiar version of the "house divided" story is found in Mark 3:21-27.[134] The scribes assert that Jesus drives out demons with power derived from the prince of demons. Good works, the scribes are contending, may conceal an evil or hostile intent.[135] A cunning antagonist may surrender or destroy something of his own in order to insinuate himself into our good graces, calculating that a small sacrifice now will lead to greater gains later on.

Jesus's response seems to deny that this tactic can succeed. Satan can only drive out Satan by being "divided against himself." But, like kingdoms and houses divided against themselves, Jesus asserts, if Satan is so divided he "cannot stand, but hath an end." This apparently naive answer reminds us of a simple truth. Satan's sacrifice of his minions does weaken his army. The satanic tactic can succeed only if we mistake the real value of things, so that we give him something of great worth in return for something less valuable, as in the folk stories in which Satan offers wealth and beauty in return for the soul. Left to itself, Satan's tactic is self-defeating; only our ignorance and confusion give it a chance of success.

Jesus goes on to make a subtler point, observing that no one can enter a strong man's house without first binding him. This is a pointed reference to the Israel of Jesus's time. In the Christian view, the Pharisees were so fearful that Israel, in the interest of accommodation with Roman and Hellenic civilization, would give up something essential to its existence as a distinct people that they insisted on the rigid observance of all rules and customs.[136] It was Jesus's violation of that code that had led the Pharisees to take counsel against him. But Pharisaism, Jesus argues, far from protecting Israel, leaves it bound and vulnerable to plunder. It makes error *certain* by raising means to the level of ends, and by confusing the accidental with the essential. A society that cannot vary its means, given the mutability of human affairs, makes its ends the prisoners of means, subordinating the greater to the less.[137] That, in fact, virtually defines a "house divided against itself." A house is not divided against itself because its members differ or have private interests; that variety is to be assumed. A house becomes divided "against itself" when what is *unlike* is regarded as more important than what is *akin*. Hence the ending of the third chapter of Mark: Jesus teaches that those who do God's will are "my brother and my sister and my mother," to be preferred, in case of conflict, to his blood kin. Private allegiances and interests must yield to public and higher goods.[138]

Political regimes and social orders—kingdoms and houses—need a measure of liberty, an element of private variation that leaves room for new ways. Yet, in Jesus's teachings, this liberty itself is only a means to the common life. It seems to me that Lincoln, reflecting on that text, saw in it the very meaning of *civil* liberty.

American institutions, as the Framers designed them, violate Jesus's teaching because they make liberty an end. Liberty is a common principle only in form; its content is radically private. What is like—the public order—is subordinated to what is unlike—the diverse and private interests of individual Americans. Consequently, America is a "house divided" *apart* from its differences about slavery, from the very first principle of its institutions. When Lincoln declared in his First Inaugural that "the Union is older than the Constitution," he was appealing to the Declaration of Independence. At Gettysburg, however, his doctrine is more mature, sharper, and more radical. The Declaration asserts that men are created equal but aim to secure their rights. At Gettysburg, Lincoln reversed that order: "Conceived" in liberty, America must be "dedicated" to equality. It amounted to the proclamation of a new covenant.[139]

Lincoln was not alone in this sort of reflection. The calamity of the Civil War shook American confidence in the Framers' science and evoked a number of attempts to apply biblical traditions to the task of reconstruction. Theorists as different as Horace Bushnell, Orestes Brownson, and Elisha Mulford, for example, agreed in rejecting individualistic ideas of natural right, in contending that human beings are naturally political, and in seeking some way to bring community into national political life.

Bushnell looked to the "little democracies of our towns . . . and legislatures" but found no institutional way to relate these small, vanishing democracies and weakened republics to the Union in the industrial era. Instead, Bushnell appealed to the argument that right rule is morally binding on us with or without our consent, a proposition that, whatever its merits, puts community in intellectual rather than affective terms.[140]

Brownson, relying on Catholic sources, found a legal formula to connect locality and nationality, asserting that sovereignty rests in the states, but in the states collectively, as parts of a whole. As Brownson knew, however, constitutional abstractions mean very little without the support of "moral qualities" rooted in political community.[141]

In Mulford's Hegelian version of the covenant, institutions are only the formalized expression of the nation, a "relationship" characterized by continuity and by a conscious, organic "moral personality." The "origins and unity" of the nation are found in the Bible, Mulford maintained. In fact, the Bible is the "book of the life of the nations" and reveals that the nations are involved in an invisible order as well as the relationships of day-to-day life. The true nation has a place in the whole of human life and history. A nation conscious of itself must be aware of the whole; this, Mulford was confident, means that self-conscious nationhood—the nation in its highest form—is necessarily Christian. The Bible, consequently, has an essential role in civic education, and Mulford lamented its absence from university curricula and its decline, in the pulpit, into so many "isolated proof texts."[142] Yet Mulford's reverence for the Bible and his belief that the accumulation of material wealth is a goal suited only to "false civilization" were insufficient to overcome his

faith in history. The highest historical forces, Mulford believed, involve sacrifice, not self-assertion; history will lead the Nation to its natural end in
God.[143]

As arguments like these suggest, Lincoln's new covenant did not prevail.
The American crisis of confidence was overridden by the end of the war and
the advent of industrial expansion. The desolation of the Civil War passed,
but what revived America was not *public* rebirth but *private* well-being. Even
those, like Bushnell, Brownson, and Mulford, who criticized the modern and
liberal foundations of American political culture were unwilling to criticize
seriously, let alone to abandon, modern political and economic institutions.
They spoke of a new spirit; they retained the old form. Yet such ideas were
not without effect: Lincoln's ideal did survive and it coexists, warringly, with
the liberal creed within American political culture. In the nineteenth century,
as Mulford's optimism suggests, such conflicts were easier to sustain than
they are today because so many Americans trusted that progress would bring
things right.

It was, in any case, a difficult time for biblical doctrine, as the Bible was
buffeted by historical criticism and evolutionary theory. There were plenty of
theologians, like Lyman Abbott, Henry Drummond, or Theodore Munger,
willing to define the Bible in evolutionary terms. The Bible, Munger wrote, is
an ''unfolding revelation'' whose laws and teachings are ''evolving their truth
and reality in the process of history.''[144] Formulations of that sort, obviously,
made it easy to dispense with biblical teaching whenever it proved inconve-
nient, most frequently in the conflict between biblical precepts and the ethics
of industrial capitalism.

The moral roots of protest, by contrast, were planted in Scripture. Leaders
like William Jennings Bryan or Walter Rauschenbusch explicitly appealed to
biblical religion, but even humanists like Henry George and Henry Demarest
Lloyd, who disclaimed their Christian beginnings, reveal the influence of biblical morality and imagery on every page. Yet even in the Social Gospel, a
good deal of the Bible's teaching has been adulterated or lost. There is almost
none of the Bible's sense of the limits to human possibility and very little of
the Bible's recognition of the moral multidimensionality of human nature.
Human meanness and destructiveness tend to be explained away, and the
stronger human loyalties are harmonized too easily with broader obligations.
The biblical tradition, in other words, showed unmistakable signs of degener-
ation into sentimentalism.[145]

The Reform Darwinism of Progressive theory drew its metaphors from the
fashionable evolutionism of the time. Yet, as Eric Goldman demonstrated, its
real lodestar was the ideal of fraternal union, an implicit absolute of political
morality.[146] In addition to its own sentimentalism, Progressive teaching
turned on a relativism that left its morality without foundation. Over time, the

argument disintegrated into the position that values and virtues are "all relative," private in principle, lacking any public dimension. Moreover, Progressives were beguiled by the notion that technology, including the "social sciences" that Progressives did so much to develop, could be shorn of its destructiveness and used to realize good ends. They rejected that most empirical
of biblical teachings, the observation that human beings are imperfect creatures, in whose hands power for good always involves power for evil.

Yet more orthodox believers have little to boast of. Embattled by the cur-
rents of social change and secularity, they have grown increasingly desperate
and they often seem more concerned to defend the Bible than they are to read
it.[147] Moreover, contemporary evangelical Christianity seems inclined to
forget, as its predecessors rarely did, that capitalism and technological change
are agents of social disintegration and moral decay. Given that error, it is not
surprising that self-proclaimed leaders of biblical orthodoxy pass over the fact
that, in Scripture, the support of the poor is a public duty.[148]

It is undeniable, however, that the influence of biblical teaching has grown
less and less powerful and articulate with the passing of time. Biblical ideas
and images remain planted in American culture and surface from time to
time—in the writings of Steinbeck and Faulkner, for example—but fewer and
fewer Americans recognize their source.[149] Even explicit references to the
Bible do not prompt many readers to reflect on the text. Nevertheless, the civil
rights movement demonstrated, even to the obtuse, the continuing political
power of the biblical tradition. And the travail of Black America has helped to
inspire more than one example of biblical wisdom.

There is no finer example of biblical influence and teaching in recent times
than James Baldwin's *Go Tell It on the Mountain*. In that novel, Baldwin is
gentle with the black church. Warts and all, the church reflects the need for
blacks to combat the white stereotype that classes them as children of nature
or, in a less benign form, as creatures of passion. The church is, as this suggests, shaped for battle with the terrible illusions of American society, of
which racism is only a symptom: a fear of vulnerability and a yearning for
mastery, a preoccupation with appearances and a blindness to the spirit.

Yet all people in the midst of battle, Baldwin comments in another context,
speak in slogans and do not want to hear complexities.[150] Moreover, warfare
makes us imitate our enemies, and the great danger of the struggle with white
society is the risk of being made over in its image. For the church, the
weapons of combat are words, its preachings and scriptural slogans, and part
of Baldwin's purpose is to indicate that words, as tools of power, corrupt the
Word, the "power which outlasts kingdoms."[151]

Three of the central characters of *Go Tell It on the Mountain*, Gabriel the
stepfather, Elizabeth the mother, and John the son, form an unmistakable allusion to the birth of John in the first chapter of Luke. There, the angel Gabriel

silences Elizabeth's husband, Zacharias, for failing to believe in Elizabeth's miraculous conception of John.[152] In the novel, Gabriel the husband is far from silent. In fact, he adopts the role of Zacharias, for he cannot see that his stepson, John, is really the child of his spirit. His eye is fixed on the child of his body, Royal. Like the America around him, Garbiel sees no further than the flesh.

Gabriel is an erstwhile preacher, and the novel relates two sermons he delivered during his heyday as an evangelist. In the first, Gabriel preached on Isaiah 6:5: "Woe is me! For I am undone, because I am a man of unclean lips and I dwell in the midst of a people of unclean lips: for mine eyes have seen the King, the Lord of hosts." His sermon is a denunciation of sin and a praise of God that emphasized the woe of unrighteous humanity. Yet Gabriel has missed the point. The text goes on to tell us that the Lord's angel seared the prophet's mouth with a live coal, purging his sin. God then calls the prophet and sends him to speak with the foreknowledge that he will not be understood. The lips of the people are not "unclean in any conventional sense: The vision of the Lord shows Isaiah that he and his people speak "uncleanly" because they speak of God in a way that debases his glory, just as Israel's ears are stopped to Isaiah's prophecy because the people will hear the words but reject their meaning.[153]

The references to uncleanliness are pointed. Isaiah tells us that his vision occurred "in the year King Uzziah died," and Uzziah died "unclean," a leper.[154] The law commands that a leper cover his lips, presumably because his very breath might pollute the community.[155] The ancient view, in other words, is that a leper is inwardly as well as outwardly unclean. The inward disease, in fact, precedes its outward signs; the leprosy, we are told, "rose up" on Uzziah's forehead, inner corruption becoming manifest to the eye.[156]

Uzziah himself was apparently pious, but his real faith lay in technology and the machinery of war. When he was strong, he was "lifted up to his destruction." He claimed that his power gave him the right to enter the sanctuary despite the prohibitions of the law, and he thus revealed that his real aim was tyrannical mastery. The Lord smote him for his presumption; Uzziah's leprosy was the outward sign of his unclean spirit.[157]

Uzziah's downfall helps explain Isaiah's vision. It is not the words Israel utters that are unclean but the spirit behind them. Like Uzziah, Israel relies on material resources, and if Israel speaks pious words, it does so largely in the hope of making God serve its own will to power. As Israel's words are inwardly tainted, so its senses are corrupted by the spirit: The eyes see and the ears hear the outward signs, but pride rejects the inner truth and refuses to understand. Like Babel, Israel sees the limits on human achievement only as obstacles to be overcome. It is doomed to defeat and exile because it requires that devastating correction.

The judgment on ancient Israel, of course, is dangerously applicable to modern America. Unwittingly, Gabriel illustrates that peril by his trivialization of the text and by his preoccupation with the sins of the flesh.

The text for Gabriel's second sermon is 2 Samuel 18:29; Ahimaaz answers David's request for "tidings" by saying, "I saw a great tumult, but I knew not what it was." Gabriel uses this as an example of the confusion of the unredeemed, and he urges his audience to know the meaning of the "tumult" so that they will be able to give the Lord "tidings" when he asks.

In this case, Gabriel's misreadings of the text is even more striking. Ahimaaz is not hesitant; he is all too eager to talk. He volunteered to bring the news of the battle to David, and he persisted in the face of Joab's warning that the king would not welcome being told that his rebellious son, Absalom, had been slain. It is only in David's presence that Ahimaaz decides to be silent. The king is more forgiving and loving than Ahimaaz realized; what is victory and a reason for jubilation for Ahimaaz is grounds for mourning for his lord. If this is true for David, how much more should we expect it to be true of the Most High? But this dimension of the story escapes Gabriel altogether. That, I suspect, is Baldwin's devastating comment on the "good news" of the church militant.

The church is too eager to speak, too unwilling to seek and wait, and at the same time, too indifferent to this world and its pain. The family home in *Go Tell It on the Mountain* is adorned with two texts: (1) an invitation—to God or guests—to come even without warning, being certain of welcome, and (2) the familiar lines of John 3:16, "And God so loved the world . . . ." These sentiments, Baldwin comments, are "somewhat unrelated," but that assertion prompts us to ask the ways in which they *are* related.[158] I think the answer to that question is found in the biblical text. God must be awaited: "No man has ascended up to heaven," but God has descended to man. Similarly, the Spirit is like the wind that blows where it wills; it can be heard but not bidden. Speaking and knowing earthly things, which human beings *can* do, take precedence over the heavenly things that are beyond the control of humankind.[159]

For the church and the polity, the care of the earth and this life must be the first items on the agenda for action. This, however, is no secular teaching. The Spirit can be *heard* if not bidden. The king's love for *all* his children is a necessary lesson for any polity, but particularly mandatory for people who, like black Americans, are justly furious at oppression. The desire for victorious retribution—Ahimaaz's tidings—needs to be silenced and humbled by the royal hope for reconciliation. The recognition of human limitations commands the church to be more political; it also insists that the polity be more spiritual. As Baldwin remarked years later, "We are meant to be witnesses to a possibility we will never see."[160]

As Baldwin knows, contemporary America is a house divided, ruled by a

Babel of private goals and armed with a technology of unparalleled potential for destruction and domination. Even very secular theorists, impressed with the "contradictions" of our life, now call for "religion," although they ordinarily intend a creed to support the established order, not biblical faith.[161] More orthodox voices are not always better advised. Today, militant believers are inclined to struggle for "nondenominational" prayer in the public schools, a policy that is possibly unconstitutional and certainly vacuous. It would make a good deal more sense to demand "nonreligious" instruction in the Bible as literature, a policy almost certainly constitutional and one with genuine content. Secular instruction in the Bible is better than none, and the Bible, as I have been arguing here, has considerable ability to take care of itself.

In any event, the articulate and silent desperation of our times is great enough that Americans may be willing to abandon some of the illusions of individualism and the quest for mastery, bringing Lincoln's new covenant closer to reality. It is also possible, of course, that America is doomed. That would be a reason for sorrow, but even so, the Bible reminds us that all regimes and peoples wither like the grass, and only the Lord endures.

Notes

1. Northrop Frye, *The Great Code: The Bible as Literature* (New York: Harcourt Brace Jovanovich, 1982).
2. When I refer to the Bible, I use the word in its most common American sense, embracing both the Jewish and Christian testaments. The idea of the "liberal tradition" is derived from Louis Hartz, *The Liberal Tradition in America* (New York: Harcourt Brace, 1955).
3. Christopher Lasch, *The Culture of Narcissism* (New York: Norton, 1978).
4. Alexis de Tocqueville, *Democracy in America* (New York: Schocken, 1961), vol. 2, pp. 118-20.
5. Nathalia Wright, *Melville's Use of the Bible* (Durham: Duke University Press, 1949); for a contemporary example, see Theodor Reik, *The Temptation* (New York: Braziller, 1961), as well as Reik's other studies of Genesis.
6. See Robert Bellah's generous discussion, "New Religious Consciousness and the Crisis of Modernity," in Bellah and Phillip Hammond, eds., *Varieties of Civil Religion* (San Francisco: Harper and Row, 1980), pp. 167-87; see also Sydney Ahlstrom, *A Religious History of the American People* (New Haven: Yale University Press, 1972), pp. 1037-54.
7. Georges Dumezil, *La religion romaine archaique* (Paris: Payot, 1966), p. 8.
8. I have, however, been, instructed by such studies; see, for example, H.H. Rowley, ed., *The Old Testament and Modern Study* (Oxford: Clarendon, 1951); Yehezekel Kaufman, *History of the Religion of Israel* (Chicago: University of Chicago Press, 1961).
9. Revelation 1:9-13; for a fine treatment of a satanic version of revelation, see James Rhodes, *The Hitler Movement* (Stanford: Hoover Institution, 1980), pp. 38-42.
10. Matthew 7:21-27; John Dillenberger, "Introduction," in *Martin Luther: Selec-*

tions from His Writings, ed. Dillenberger (Garden City, NY: Doubleday, 1961), p. 19. Robin Needham argues a similar point in "Terminology and Alliance," *Sociologus* 16 (1966): 156-57, and 17 (1967): 47-50.

11. Martin Buber, *On the Bible*, ed. Nahum Glatzer (New York: Schocken, 1968), p. 5.

12. Exodus 34:9; Deuteronomy 9:6, 10:16, 30:14; Ezekiel 2:4, 8.

13. Deuteronomy 32:46-47.

14. Perry Miller, *Nature's Nation* (Cambridge: Harvard University Press, 1967), pp. 214-15, 220; see also Dillenberger, *Martin Luther: Selections*, p. 474.

15. Deuteronomy 32:46-47.

16. Hence, Torah is "didactic-historical instruction" as much as—or more than—a set of specific laws and regulations. Calum Carmichael, *The Laws of Deuteronomy* (Ithaca, NY: Cornell University Press, 1974), p. 18, n. 3.

17. 2 Timothy 3:15; on wisdom and Scripture, see Leo Strauss, *Jerusalem and Athens*, City College Papers #6 (New York: City College of New York, 1967), p. 5.

18. John 20:30-31; Carmichael, *Laws of Deuteronomy*, p. 7; George Mendenhall, *The Tenth Generation* (Baltimore: Johns Hopkins University Press, 1973), p. 8. Solomon Goldman's comment, "The Book of Genesis is the great clearing which the fashioners of the Jewish saga made in the jungle of primitive folklore," speaks to the point. *The Book of Human Destiny* (New York: Harper, 1949), p. xi.

19. Edmund Leach, *Genesis as Myth and Other Essays* (London: Jonathan Cape, 1969), pp. 29-30; Julius Wellhausen, *Prolegomena to the History of Ancient Israel* (New York: Meridian, 1957; orig. 1878). Spinoza anticipated this argument. See Leo Strauss, *Spinoza's Critique of Religion* (New York: Schocken, 1965), p. 267.

20. Buber, *On the Bible*, p. 36; Buber, of course, is speaking of the Jewish scriptures, but because Christian authors were concerned to show that the New Testament fulfills the Old, they were no less concerned with unity of composition. (See Franz Rosenzweig, *Star of Redemption* [New York: Holt, Rinehart and Winston, 1971], p. 117.) Strauss appears to reject this view. The compilers of the Bible, Strauss asserts, "seem" to have "excluded only what could not by any stretch of the imagination be rendered compatible with the fundamental and authoritative teaching." Hence, unlike a "book in the strict sense," the contradictions and repetitions in the Bible may not be intended (*Jerusalem and Athens*, p. 18). Strauss does not tell us the evidence for this view, but he concedes that the "traditional way of reading the Bible" *does* treat it as a "book in the strict sense" (ibid., p. 19). It is apparently a fair assumption that Strauss's nontraditional view is based on a modern reading, on things as they "seem" in the light of the historical criticism of Scripture. This principle of interpretation is curious because Strauss so often cautions his readers against historicistic readings, and especially because he lays down the rule that "it is safer to understand the low in the light of the high than the high in the light of low. In doing the latter one necessarily distorts the high, whereas in doing the former, one does not deprive the low of the freedom to reveal itself fully as what it is" (*Spinoza's Critique of Religion*, p. 2; see also pp. 7-8, 12-14, 21-25, and "On Collingwood's Philosophy of History," *Review of Metaphysics* 5 [1952]: 559-86). Since it is unlikely that Strauss contradicted himself on so important a point in relation to so important a text, the safest assumption is that Strauss's approach to the Bible is

compatible with his exegetic precepts. This is possible if (1) the view that the Bible is not a "book in the strict sense" is true to the *highest* possibilities of Scripture, and (2) that his view of the way in which the Bible's editors selected their texts is not a historicistic reading but reflects the way in which those editors understood themselves. In fact, Strauss's seemingly modern view itself emphasizes that Scripture's editors *had* a guiding purpose, a "fundamental and authoritative teaching." Moreover, Strauss is contending that Scripture's accounts and stories are compatible with this teaching, although we must sometimes stretch our imaginations to discern that compatibility. Closely examined, in other words, Strauss's argument maintains something like the traditional view: The Bible is not a "book in the strict sense" only because its fundamental teachings and unities are more difficult to discover. This is as it should be. The Bible claims to speak about divine things; God is the unity underlying Scripture. Human speech, however, must fall short of God, the Word that is the foundation of all language yet beyond all words. If the Bible is not a "book in the strict sense," it may be because it is written in an even stricter sense, with an understanding of the limitations of books and writings. (I find something like this view in Chaim Potok's essay, "The Bible's Inspired Art," *New York Times Magazine,* Oct. 3, 1982, pp. 58ff.)

21. 1 Samuel 31:4; 2 Samuel 1:6-10.
22. Herbert N. Schneidau, *Sacred Discontent: The Bible and Western Tradition* (Berkeley and Los Angeles: University of California Press, 1977), pp. 214-15.
23. Carmichael, *Laws of Deuteronomy,* pp. 23, 256-57.
24. Henry David Thoreau, *Walden,* ed. J. Lyndon Shanley (Princeton: Princeton University Press, 1971), pp. 106, 100, and pp. 99-110 passim. Thoreau's unorthodox inclusion of other sacred works along with the Bible does not make him less insistent on applying his principles of interpretation to the Bible: see also Buber, *On the Bible,* pp. 30, 213, and the comments on stretching the imagination in n. 20 above.
25. Wright, *Melville's Use of the Bible,* pp. 12-13, 17-18, 45, 114-15; see also my *Idea of Fraternity in America* (Berkeley and Los Angeles: University of California Press, 1973), pp. 317-18, 331-32.
26. Dillenberger, *Martin Luther: Selections,* p. 343; Jacques Ellul, *The Politics of God and the Politics of Man* (Grand Rapids, MI: Eerdmans, 1972), p. 113.
27. Buber, *On the Bible,* p. 1; Rosenzweig, *Star of Redemption,* pp. 198-204.
28. Miller, *Nature's Nation,* pp. 216, 219, 222, 234.
29. Exodus 20:4; Isaiah 40:15-25; Peter L. Berger, *The Noise of Solemn Assemblies* (Garden City, NY: Doubleday, 1961), p. 131; Henri Frankfort et al., *Before Philosophy* (Baltimore: Penguin, 1961), p. 243.
30. Georges Dumezil, *The Destiny of the Warrior* (Chicago: University of Chicago Press, 1970), p. 3; Mendenhall, *Tenth Generation,* pp. 7, 16.
31. Peter L. Berger, *The Sacred Canopy* (Garden City, NY: Doubleday, 1969), pp. 99, 112-24; Eric Voegelin, *Israel and Revelation* (Baton Rouge: Louisiana State University Press, 1966).
32. This, of course, helps account for the extraordinary capacity for self-criticism in the biblical tradition. For example, see Jeremiah 7:26; Ezekiel 20:25-26; on the general point, see Mendenhall, *Tenth Generation,* p. 15; Schneidau, *Sacred Discontent,* p. 14; Peter L. Berger, *The Precarious Vision* (Garden City, NY: Doubleday, 1961), pp. 219ff.; Frank M. Cross, *Canaanite Myth and Hebrew Epic* (Cambridge: Harvard University Press, 1973), pp. 89-90, 190-91.

33. Frankfort et al., *Before Philosophy*, pp. 241-43; the italics are theirs.
34. Genesis 1:31.
35. Buber, *On the Bible*, p. 195, commenting on Job 38:4-5, 9-10. Herbert Schneidau has a point in arguing that the Bible's attack on "the old mythology of the community and its culture" helps to lay the "groundwork" for the "mythology of the individual," so long as it is understood that this second mythology is no less contrary to the Bible's teaching than the first (*Sacred Discontent*, p. 45).
36. Psalms 103:15-16; see also Ecclesiastes 1:11, 13.
37. Isaiah 64:6; John 2:19.
38. Isaiah 40:6-11, 29-31.
39. Mendenhall, *Tenth Generation*, pp. xii-xiii, 5.
40. Schneidau, *Sacred Discontent*, p. 154.
41. Genesis 4:7.
42. Genesis 4:12-15.
43. Genesis 4:17.
44. A.M. Hocart, *Kings and Councillors* (Chicago: University of Chicago Press, 1970), pp. 35, 38.
45. This helps to account for the Bible's deep and continuing suspicion of commerce and money. 1 Timothy 6:10; Genesis 47:15-18, Exodus 22:25; Deuteronomy 23:19; Psalms 49:5-10; Jeremiah 9:23; Mark 10:23-25; James 4:13-56.
46. A.L. Oppenheim, *Ancient Mesopotamia* (Chicago: University of Chicago Press, 1964), pp. 82-83; Mendenhall, *Tenth Generation*, pp. 105-10, and "The Hebrew Conquest of Palestine," in *The Biblical Archaeologist Reader*, ed. E.F. Campbell and David Freedman (Garden City, NY: Doubleday, 1970), pp. 103, 105.
47. Genesis 11:4.
48. Compare Robin Needham, "Editor's Introduction," in Hocart, *Kings and Councillors*, p. xxx.
49. Carmichael, *Laws of Deuteronomy*, pp. 261-62; see also Buber's discussion of the distinction between a people defined by biology or history (*goy*) and a community (*am*) (*On the Bible*, pp. 85-86).
50. John Bright, *History of Israel* (London: SCM Press, 1967), pp. 132-37; see also Werner Muller, *Die heilige Stadt* (Stuttgart: Kohlhammer, 1961).
51. Genesis 8:21, 9:2.
52. This goes beyond material possessions because it includes "my ideas."
53. Proverbs 28:1; Ecclesiastes 4:7-14; John Hallowell, *The Moral Foundations of Democracy* (Chicago: University of Chicago Press, 1954), pp. 99-100.
54. Genesis 1:31; 50:19-20; Deuteronomy 30:14.
55. Buber, *On the Bible*, pp. 13, 87.
56. Genesis 50:20; see also Genesis 15:12-15, 21:1, 22:1-12, 33:3-4, 41:41, 45:28.
57. Buber, *On the Bible*, pp. 36-43; Genesis 13:9-9, 20:9-11; Schneidau, *Sacred Discontent*, pp. 133-34; Bright, *History of Israel*, p. 135.
58. Deuteronomy 10:18, 15:7-11.
59. Buber, *On the Bible*, pp. 109-10.
60. Reinhold Niebuhr, *Moral Man and Immoral Society* (New York: Schribner's 1932).
61. Genesis 18:17-33, 19:1-23.
62. Genesis 12:1, 24:4, 14, 17-21.
63. Genesis 40:12-19, 41:25-37, 47:13-21.

64. Compare the similar experience of the Babylonian exile: Bright, *History of Israel*, pp. 415-20.

65. Buber, *On the Bible*, pp. 85-86; Augustine, *City of God*, Book 4, ch. 3, 15, Book 5, ch. 12, 17, Book 19, ch. 12, 21ff. Lassa Oppenheim favors the modernized version of Christianity, which teaches that "the principles of Christianity ought to unite Christians more than they have done hitherto," but he admits that applying this precept to the case for an international regime requires that "the letter" of Christian religion—its biblical principles—yield to its "spirit" (*International Law*, 3d ed. [London: Longmans Green, 1920], vol. 1, pp. 60-61). On the development of this question in Christian thought, see Ewart K. Lewis, *Medieval Political Ideas* (London: Routledge and Kegan Paul, 1954), vol. 2, pp. 430-66.

66. Isaiah 40:17; Psalms 2:10-11, 47:7-9; Martin Buber, *The Kingdom of God* (New York: Harper, 1967).

67. Jeremiah 1:10.

68. Buber, *On the Bible*, p. 170; see also pp. 166-71.

69. Jonah 5:2.

70. Compare Socrates's teaching as Plato presents it in *Apology*, 25c5-26e6, and *Republic* 335d.

71. On the other hand, Puritanism and the common law often followed parallel courses: see David Little, *Religion, Order and Law* (New York: Harper and Row, 1969). One relatively late example of the appeal to the Bible as the foundation of law is Lyman Beecher, *The Bible: A Code of Laws* (Andover, MA: Flagg and Gould, 1818).

72. John Winthrop, *The Winthrop Papers* (Boston: Massachusetts Historical Society, 1929-1947), vol. 2, pp. 282-95; John Cotton, *An Exposition of the Thirteenth Chapter of Revelations* (London, 1656), p. 121; H. Richard Niebuhr, *The Kingdom of God in America* (Chicago: Willet, 1937), pp. 59-62, and "The Idea of Covenant and American Democracy," *Church History* 23 (1954): 129.

73. For some recent studies, see Richard Gildrie, *Salem, Massachusetts, 1629-1688: A Covenant Community* (Charlottesville: University of Virginia Press, 1975); Stephen Foster, *Their Solitary Way* (New Haven: Yale University Press, 1971); David Leverenz, *The Language of Puritan Feeling* (New Brunswick: Rutgers University Press, 1980); Ernest B. Lowrie, *The Shape of the Puritan Mind* (New Haven: Yale University Press, 1974); Emory Elliott, *Power and the Pulpit in Puritan New England* (Princeton: Princeton University Press, 1975).

74. Alan Heimert, *Religion and the American Mind* (Cambridge: Harvard University Press, 1966), pp. 352-53; see also Robert Bellah, *Beyond Belief* (New York: Harper and Row, 1970), pp. 187-88.

75. Bellah and Hammond, *Varieties of Civil Religion*, p. 11.

76. John H. Schaar, "Some Ways of Thinking About Equality," *Journal of Politics* 26 (1964): 867-95; that the three attributes (or "persons") of God mentioned in the Declaration correspond to the three powers of government underlines, in my view, the extent to which the Creator of the Declaration is a civil rather than a biblical deity. (See Harry V. Jaffa, "What Is Equality?" in *The Conditions of Freedom* [Baltimore: Johns Hopkins University Press, 1975], p. 153.)

77. Isaiah 14:12-15.

78. *The Federalist* 10, 51; Gordon Wood, *The Creation of the American Republic* (Chapel Hill: University of North Carolina Press, 1969), p. 429, citing the *Boston Independent Chronicle*, Nov. 2, 1786; Thomas Jefferson, *Works*, Federal ed.

(New York: Putnam's, 1904), vol. 12, p. 477; Martin Diamond, "Ethics and Politics: The American Way," in *The Moral Foundations of the American Republic*, ed. Robert Horwitz (Charlottesville: University of Virginia Press, 1977), pp. 39-72.

79. Walter Berns, "Religion and the Principle," in Horwitz, *Moral Foundations of the American Republic*, pp. 163-64, 170; see also Thomas Pangle, *Montesquieu's Philosophy of Liberalism* (Chicago: University of Chicago Press, 1973), pp. 249-59. Sidney Mead writes that "every Species of traditional orthodoxy in Christendom is at war with the basic premises upon which the constitutional and legal structures of the Republic rest." *Old Religion in the Brave New World* (Berkeley and Los Angeles: University of California Press, 1977), p. 2.

80. Gaillard Hunt, ed., *The Writings of James Madison* (New York: Putnam's, 1900-1910), vol. 9, p. 220; vol. 2, pp. 183-91. Madison felt, in fact, that it would constitute an "establishment of religion" if the census counted ministers. Mark De Wolfe Howe, *The Garden and the Wilderness* (Chicago: University of Chicago Press, 1965), p. 62.

81. A.E. Dick Howard, *Commentaries on the Constitution of Virginia* (Charlottesville: University of Virginia Press, 1974), vol. 1, pp. 290-93; see also Irving Brant, "Madison on the Separation of Church and State," *William and Mary Quarterly* 8, 3d series (1951): 3, 15-16, 23-24.

82. Gordon Wood, "The Democratization of Mind in the American Revolution," in Horwitz, *Moral Foundations of the American Republic*, p. 111.

83. Thomas Paine, *Common Sense and Other Political Writings*, ed. N. Adkins (New York: Liberal Arts, 1953), p. 10.

84. Exodus 28:5-12.

85. Schneidau, *Sacred Discontent*, p. 244.

86. Paine, *Common Sense*, p. 32.

87. Ibid., pp. 13-14.

88. Ibid., p. 51; it is almost certainly significant that Paine relegated this reference to beginning the world again to the appendix to *Common Sense*. The choice of Saul is referred to at p. 15.

89. Ibid., p. 25; John Milton, *Paradise Lost*, iv, 98-99.

90. Heimert, *Religion and the American Mind*, p. 479.

91. Mead, *Old Religion in the Brave New World*, p. 5.

92. Berns "Religion and the Founding Principle," pp. 165-66; Wood, *Creation of the American Republic*, pp. 427-28.

93. Thomas Jefferson, *Notes on the State of Virginia*, ed. W. Peden (Chapel Hill: University of North Carolina Press, 1955), pp. 159, 162-63; Harvey Mansfield, Jr., "Introduction," in *Thomas Jefferson: Selected Writings*, ed. Mansfield (Arlington Heights, IL: AHM Publishing, 1979), p. xxvi; on Jefferson's idea of "Heart," see his letter to Mrs. Cosway, in *Life and Selected Writings of Thomas Jefferson*, ed. A. Koch and William Peden (New York: Modern Library, 1944), pp. 395-407. John Chester Miller, *The Wolf by the Ears* (New York: Free Press, 1977), is an excellent study of Jefferson's views on slavery.

94. Jefferson, *Works*, vol. 9, p. 461; Jefferson, *Notes on the State of Virginia*, p. 148. See also S. Gerald Sandler, "Lockean Ideas in Jefferson's *Bill for Establishing Religious Freedom*," *Journal of the History of Ideas* 21 (1960): 110-16.

95. Wood, "The Democratization of Mind," p. 114; Donald Stewart, *The Opposition Press of the Federalist Period* (Albany: State University of New York Press, 1969), pp. 15, 624, 634, 638, 640.

96. Eldon Eisenach, "The American Revolution Made and Remembered," *American Studies*, Spring 1979, p. 77; Mary Kelley and Sidney Mead, "Protestantism in the Shadow of the Enlightenment," *Soundings* 58 (1975): 335-38.

97. Isaac Backus, "An Appeal to the Public for Religious Liberty," in *Isaac Backus on Church, State and Calvinism: Pamphlets 1754-1789*, ed. William G. McLoughlin (Cambridge: Harvard University Press, 1968), pp. 305-6, 328.

98. William G. McLoughlin, *Isaac Backus and the American Pietistic Tradition* (Boston: Little, Brown, 1951), pp. 149, 212.

99. William G. McLoughlin, "Isaac Backus and the Separation of Church and State in America," *American Historical Review* 73 (1968): 1392-1413; Samuel Adams, *Writings*, ed. H.A. Cushing (New York: Putnam's, 1908), vol. 4, p. 238; see also vol. 3, p. 163.

100. Rhys Isaac, "Preachers and Patriots: Popular Culture and Revolution in Virginia," in *The American Revolution*, ed. Alfred Young (De Kalb: Northern Illinois University Press, 1976), pp. 125-50; Elisha Douglass, *Rebels and Democrats* (Chicago: Quadrangle, 1965), pp. 115-61.

101. Heimert, *Religion and the American Mind*, pp. 95, 140, 179-82, 403; Tocqueville, of course, later endorsed this view: *Democracy in America*, vol. 1, p. 383.

102. Heimert, *Religion and the American Mind*, pp. 32, 55, 87, 381, 496-97.

103. Ibid., p. 306; see also pp. 298-99, 515-17.

104. Ibid., pp. 40, 265, 455-56, 459, 468, 504. For a fine example of the political thought of the Awakening, see Nathaniel Niles, *Two Discourses on Liberty* (Newbury-Port, MA: Thomas Tinges, 1774).

105. Heimert, *Religion and the American Mind*, p. 526.

106. Herbert Schneider, *The Puritan Mind* (New York: Holt, 1930), pp. 106-10; Heimert, *Religion and the American Mind*, p. 15; Richard Birdsall, "The Second Great Awakening and New England Social Order," *Church History* 39 (1970): 345. On Edwards's rather different personal views, see Heimert, *Religion and the American Mind*, p. 129, and Perry Miller, *Jonathan Edwards* (New York: Delta, 1949), pp. 214-32.

107. Jonathan Edwards, *Religious Affections* (New Haven: Yale University Press, 1959), p. 300.

108. Heimert, *Religion and the American Mind*, p. 225; H.R. Niebuhr, *Kingdom of God in America*, p. 109.

109. Romans 10:12; Galatians 3:28; 1 John 4:21; Thessalonians 4:9-11.

110. Heimert, *Religion and the American Mind*, pp. 61-68, 190; Nathan Hatch, *The Sacred Cause of Liberty* (New Haven: Yale University Press, 1977).

111. Heimert, *Religion and the American Mind*, pp. 288, 395-97.

112. Ibid., pp. 104-5; Harvey G. Townsend, *The Philosophy of Jonathan Edwards* (Eugene: University of Oregon Press, 1955), p. 65.

113. Van Wyck Brooks, *The Flowering of New England* (New York: Dutton, 1936), pp. 59-60; G.K. Chesterton, *What I Saw in America* (New York: Dodd, Mead, 1922), pp. 16-17; William Sullivan, *Reconstructing Public Philosophy* (Berkeley and Los Angeles: University of California Press, 1982), p. 13.

114. Perry Miller, *The Life of the Mind in America* (New York: Harcourt, Brace and World, 1965), pp. 3-95; Heimert, *Religion and the American Mind*, pp. 546-52.

115. Heimert, *Religion and the American Mind*, pp. vii, 534; Miller, *Nature's Nation*, pp. 208-40.

116. Tocqueville, *Democracy in America*, vol. 1, pp. 355-73; vol. 2, pp. 22-32.

117. Schneidau, *Sacred Discontent*, p. 56; compare Roland Barthes, *Mythologies* (New York: Hill and Wang, 1972).
118. Berger, *Noise of Solemn Assemblies*, pp. 57-72, 112, 117; John Murray Cuddihy, *No Offense: Civil Religion and Protestant Taste* (New York: Seabury, 1978).
119. Cited, Ahlstrom, *Religious History of the American People*, p. 399.
120. See my discussion in *Idea of Fraternity in America*, pp. 283-84; Randall Stewart, *American Literature and Christian Doctrine* (Baton Rouge: Louisiana State University Press, 1958), pp. 43-65.
121. McWilliams, *Idea of Fraternity in America*, pp. 282-89, 304-18, 338-42; Quentin Anderson, *The Imperial Self* (New York: Knopf, 1971), pp. 3-87.
122. Herman Melville, *Israel Potter: His Fifty Years of Exile* (New York: Sagamore, 1957), pp. 63, 74; Miller, *Nature's Nation*, p. 223.
123. Genesis 46:30, 47:9, 48:8-11, 49.
124. The King James version translates Genesis 48:21 as "Behold, I die." Jacob does not die until 49:33.
125. See my discussion of Melville's ideas in *Idea of Fraternity in America*, pp. 328-71.
126. Caleb Sprague Henry, *Considerations on Some of the Elements and Conditions of Social Welfare and Human Progress* (New York: Appleton, 1861), pp. 220-26, 238-39, 241-42, 290.
127. John H. Schaar, "Jacques Ellul: Between Babylon and the New Jerusalem," *Democracy* 2, no. 4 (Fall 1982): 102-18.
128. 1 Corinthians 7:21; see also Ephesians 6:6-7.
129. Genesis 9:25; on scientific racism, see McWilliams, *Idea of Fraternity in America*, pp. 258, 253-70 passim.
130. Deuteronomy 23:15.
131. Henry S. Commager, *Theodore Parker* (Boston: Beacon, 1960), p. 216. This, at least, was Parker's report of the incident.
132. H.R. Niebuhr, *Kingdom of God in America*, pp. 156-59; Melville made much the same point in *Benito Cereno*.
133. For a challenging commentary on Lincoln's speech, see Harry V. Jaffa, *Crisis of the House Divided* (Seattle: University of Washington Press, 1973; orig. 1959).
134. The other versions differ only in context, although this matters a good deal. Matthew, for example, preceded the story with a reference to the prophecies of Isaiah and his own attribution to Jesus of descent from David (12:17-23), and Matthew follows the story by a foretelling of Jesus's death and resurrection (12:40). Matthew, in other words, is concerned to establish the preeminent authority of Jesus, and places the story of the "divided house" within that context. Mark, by contrast, tells the story in relation to Jesus's ordination of his disciples (3:14-19), a much more egalitarian setting.
135. Jesus himself makes this argument: Matthew 7:22.
136. Bright, *History of Israel*, pp. 423, 427.
137. Mark 2:27, 3:4.
138. Mark 3:32-35.
139. Bellah, *Beyond Belief*, pp. 177-78.
140. Horace Bushnell, *Building Eras in Religion* (New York: Scribner's, 1910; orig. 1864), pp. 293-95, 298, 309, 317.
141. Orestes Brownson, *The American Republic*, ed. A.D. Lapati (New Haven, CT: Colleges and Universities Press, 1972), pp. 27, 31-34, 98, 102.

142. Elisha Mulford, *The Nation* (Boston: Houghton Mifflin, 1887), pp. v-vi, 5-23, 382-83, 390-91.
143. Elisha Mulford, *The Republic of God* (Boston: Houghton Mifflin, 1881), p. 189; Mulford, *Nation*, pp. 319, 381, 395, 408.
144. Theodore Munger, *The Freedom of Faith* (Boston: Houghton Mifflin, 1883), pp. 19ff.; Lyman Abbott, *The Theology of an Evolutionist* (New York: Houghton Mifflin, 1897) and *The Evolution of Christianity* (Boston: Houghton Mifflin, 1892); Henry Drummond, *The Ascent of Man* (New York: Pott. 1894). For a contemporay version of this argument, see Thomas J.J. Altizer, *The Gospel of Christian Atheism* (Philadelphia: Westminister, 1966), pp. 27-28, 77.
145. McWilliams, *Idea of Fraternity in America*, pp. 383-88, 402-6, 479-83.
146. Eric Goldman, *Rendezvous with Destiny* (New York: Knopf, 1954), pp. 93-94, 200.
147. The most notable omission is the failure to read seriously the account of creation in Genesis 1. To do so is to recognize that creation days are not necessarily identical to sun days, and certainly not on the authority of the text (Strauss, *Jerusalem and Athens*, pp. 8-9; see also Anne Brennan, "The Creationist Controversy: The Religious Issue," *Commonweal* 109 [1982]: 559-61). On the more general shortcomings of the religious right, see Gabriel Fackre, *The Religious Right and Christian Faith* (Grand Rapids MI: Eerdmans, 1982).
148. For one example, see Arthur Hallaman, *Christian Capitalism* (Akron, Ohio: Capitalist Press, 1981). By contrast, see Bob Goudzwaard, *Capitalism and Progress: A Diagnosis of Western Society*, trans. J. Zylstra (Grand Rapids, MI: Eerdmans, 1979); see also John H. Schaar, *Legitimacy in the Modern State* (New Brunswick: Transaction Books, 1981).
149. Stewart, *American Literature and Christian Doctrine*, pp. 136-46, has a good discussion of Faulkner and Robert Penn Warren.
150. Carolyn Wedin Sylvander, *James Baldwin* (New York: Ungar, 1980), p. 21.
151. James Baldwin, *Nobody Knows My Name* (New York: Delta, 1962), p. 233.
152. Luke 1:20.
153. Isaiah 6:9.
154. Isaiah 6:1; 2 Chronicles 29:21.
155. Leviticus 13:45.
156. 2 Chronicles 29:19
157. 2 Chronicles 29:9-20.
158. James Baldwin, *Go Tell It on the Mountain* (New York: Dell, 1965), p. 28.
159. John 3:8, 12, 13.
160. James Baldwin and Margaret Mead, *A Rap on Race* (Philadelphia: Lippincott, 1971), p. 201.
161. Daniel Bell, *The Cultural Contradictions of Capitalism* (New York: Basic Books, 1976); Michael Novak, *The Spirit of Democratic Capitalism* (New York: Simon and Schuster, 1982).

3

The Dilemma of Reconciling
Traditional, Cultural, and Political
Needs: Civil Religion in Israel

Charles S. Liebman
Eliezer Don-Yehia

There are two models or conceptions of the primary function of modern governments. We call one the service model. According to this model, the function of government is to provide services and to reconcile conflicting interests among groups and individuals. David Apter uses the term *reconciliation system* to describe the "secular-libertarian" form of authority that generally characterizes such a state (Apter 1965:25). He contrasts it with what he calls a mobilization system characterized by a "sacred collectivity" form of authority. This fits, with some modification, what we call a visionary model. In this model, government has a predetermined vision or goal, and its primary function is to educate and mobilize on the vision's behalf. The term *vision* is appropriate because a goal transcends the immediate material needs of the nation's population, which is conceived as a moral community.

Our models stand at two ends of a theoretical continuum and are useful in distinguishing between governments that fall closer to one or the other end. Clearly governments of the Soviet Union or Nazi Germany or Cuba are closer to the visionary end of the continuum, and Sweden or England to the service end. But the service model is not necessarily more democratic or the visionary one more authoritarian. It depends to some extent on whom the government services and who generates and shares the vision (the elite or the entire population). There is a tendency for visionary governments to adopt authoritarian means, but this tendency may be restrained by other aspects of the political culture. Robert Bellah, for example, distinguishes a liberal constitutional regime from a republic. Liberal constitutionalism (a service-type model) is built on the notion that "a good society can result from the actions of citizens motivated by self-interest alone when those actions are organized through proper mechanisms." The republic (a visionary-democratic type model) "has an ethical, educational, even spiritual role . . ." (Bellah 1980:9).

The foregoing suggests a four-celled matrix of modern nation-states.

Democratic

Service	A	B	Visionary
State	C	D	State

Authoritarian

Type A, the service-democratic model, and Type D, the visionary-authoritarian model, are more common types of regimes, but Type C, the service-authoritarian model (e.g., Jordan), and Type B, the visionary-democratic model (e.g., Israel), do exist in reality as well as in theory.

One would anticipate that any visionary government would develop a highly articulated system of symbols (rituals, myths, special terminology, shrines, heroic figures, and the like) that defines the boundaries and the meaning of the moral community, legitimates the vision, socializes the population to the values it embodies, and mobilizes the population to the efforts required for its realization. This is what we mean by the term *civil religion*.

Civil religion, in turn, can be primarily political or social in its orientation (Wilson 1979, for a similar distinction). Where the orientation is primarily political, the vision is generated and imposed by an elite; the symbols point to the centrality of the state; power and national unity are emphasized; and the structure of government tends to be authoritative, although, as we shall see, even this is compatible with a democratic regime.

Where the orientation is primarily social, the vision emerges as a collective conception and its parameters and meaning are defined by a variety of groups, each of which adds its own nuances; the symbols point to the society and its people rather than to the state; voluntarism and pluralism are valued more than power and unity; and the structure of government tends to be democratic rather than authoritarian.

Our concern is civil religion's approach to a problem endemic to all new nations: the relationship between the needs of the nation and the tradition(s) and culture(s) from which the new nation emerged. One can construct a civil religion out of new or syncretic symbols, denying that the civil religion is connected to a past tradition. There are problems with this option. Part of the population may be deeply committed to its own tradition and perceive that tradition as bearing implications for the conduct of the nation. In addition, the leaders of the new nation will want to exploit traditional symbols and values to strengthen national loyalties among this segment of the population. Furthermore, even among the more modern (secular) elements of the population, some primordial ties are likely to be retained, and the traditional culture offers the new nation a sense of continuity with the past. This may serve to legitimate the people's right to the land itself, to autonomy, and to an identity as a group distinct from others.

On the other hand, even if we assume only one tradition, some people may be ideologically as well as behaviorally nontraditional, if not antitraditional. Hence, traditional symbols may be divisive rather than integrative, delegitimating instead of legitimating. Second, values and behavior patterns anchored in traditional culture may hinder efforts at reorganization and change in political, economic, and social spheres.[1]

The problem is particularly acute in visionary-democratic states. Service states avoid the purposive shaping of their political culture. In the visionary-authoritarian state (all totalitarian states fall into this category), the political elite views the tradition, particularly when it is institutionalized in traditional religion, as a competitor for loyalty and an obstacle in its effort to shape the society in accordance with its values. Hence, totalitarian regimes develop new symbols that they hope will integrate and mobilize the population and legitimate their political vision. All the instruments of a modern state stand at their disposal in this effort. But under special conditions, in times of crisis in particular, even totalitarian regimes may rely on traditional symbols. In that case they confront the dilemma of reconciling their political needs with the values inherent in traditional culture—a dilemma that visionary-democratic states confront most acutely—because they lack the coercive instrumentalities of the authoritarian regime. The very condition of political freedom and the possibility of cultural pluralism makes tradition an especially attractive source for symbols because of the deference in which it is held. This is especially true where the majority of the population views itself as the heirs of one tradition, and that tradition speaks in one way or another to matters of national concern. The dilemma arises, as we noted, from the presence of one or more dissenting minorities, but even in their absence, from the inappropriateness of traditional symbols and values to the political needs of a modern state. Hence, the effort by democratic visionary states to resolve the dilemma by transforming and transvaluing traditional symbols to make them more compatible to dissenting minorities and to the needs of the state. Obviously, the dilemma can never be entirely resolved because the more the symbols are transformed and transvalued to overcome one horn of the dilemma, the less "traditional" they become. Symbols are continually transformed and transvalued in traditional culture as well. The difference is in the degree and self-consciousness of the transformation and transvaluation. We distinguish three approaches or strategies of transformation and transvaluation in visionary-democratic regimes:

Confrontation. In the first approach, the civil religion self-consciously confronts and to some degree rejects the tradition, but it forms its symbols out of this rejection. The link to the tradition is maintained by the very seriousness that is accorded to traditional symbols that are deliberately changed in order to adapt them to new needs and values. This approach is particularly suited to culturally sophisticated people among whom the tradition is too deeply embedded to be ignored but who have rejected many of its symbols and/or their referents.

It is not easy to sustain a confrontation approach in a pluralistic-democratic polity where a considerable part of the population is traditionalist. A civil religion that is based exclusively on such an approach is likely to be a divisive rather than an integrative force in society. Hence over the long run this approach can be maintained as one variant in a civil religion that makes room for other approaches or strategies as well.

Selectionism. The second approach, which we call selectionism, maintains that the tradition is composed of a variety of strands reflecting different sets of symbols and values. Some of these are affirmed and others are ignored, rather than confronted and rejected. Selectivity, it is argued, is quite legitimate within the context of the tradition itself. In fact, some proponents of this approach claim that the part of the tradition that they affirm is really more legitimate, authentic, or essential than that which they reject.

This approach is associated with a system of beliefs and symbols that aspires to become the common civil religion of the whole polity. Such a civil religion tends to stress the importance of that which unites the nation, such as the state and its institutions. Hence, the association between the selectionist approach and a civil religion whose orientation is primarily political rather than social.

Reinterpretation. The third approach nominally affirms the entire tradition. The civil religion associated with this approach is characterized by the penetration of traditional symbols throughout the culture and their reinterpretation so that new values may be imposed upon them. As we observed, all religious development is characterized by reinterpretation and imposition of new values. The distinction is really the degree to which traditional symbols are reinterpreted to meet contemporary needs.

This is the least self-conscious of all approaches and is closest, in structure as well as content, to traditional religion. The attitude toward the tradition is very positive. Were the adherents of the reinterpretation approach to admit to their transvaluation of traditional symbols, they would transform them into arbitrary signs devoid of meaning and defeat the very purpose they seek to achieve: legitimating their values by linking them to the tradition. The reinterpretation approach is encouraged by a decline in the influence of a modern-secular belief systems and their capacity to legitimate societal institutions and values.

The Case of Israel

Israel is a visionary-democratic type of society, and the nature of its vision provides two dimensions to the dilemma of reconciling traditional culture and contemporary political needs.

First, Zionism is the vision around which Jewish society in the Land of Israel formed itself. According to this vision, Jews, through their own efforts will construct a Jewish society in their own land that will be the cultural and political center of all Jews. This is a basic component of Israeli civil religion in all its manifestations. To confirm the Jewish identity of the Israeli polity (and the polity of the *yishuv*—the modern prestate Jewish settlement in Palestine), Zionist civil religion required symbols drawn from traditional Jewish culture capable of expressing and fostering the historic and contemporary links among Judaism, the Jewish people, and the Israeli polity.

In view of the central role of Jewish religion in the national history and culture of the Jewish people, there is hardly a single Jewish symbol that is not loaded with religious meaning. The problem is more than the fact that broad circles in Israeli society are overtly secularist; they might simply accept the symbols as part of their historical heritage. The problem is the references and meanings to which the symbols point. The Jewish religion is God-centered. It accords ultimate power and authority in human affairs, including those of a social and political nature, to God alone. God is the only true king of Israel, its sole protector and redeemer. It is not easy to reconcile this point of view with a conception of national self-redemption, which is a central component of modern Zionism.

This can be illustrated by reference to problems involved in the celebration of Jewish holidays. Passover and Hannukah (the feast of lights) are among the most widely celebrated Jewish holidays. Both have explicit national historical referents: Passover commemorates the Jewish exodus from Egypt; Hannukah, the Maccabean or Hasmonean revolt and the attainment of cultic freedom and a large measure of Jewish sovereignty in the Second Temple period.

Both Passover and Hannukah, one might expect, would serve as important components in Israeli civil religion providing mythic-ritual symbols that would remind Israelis of their heroic past, of their lengthy history, their having overcome vicissitudes, and so on. The problem is that the holidays have assumed a fairly specific meaning in the Jewish tradition and subsymbols were developed or interpreted in accordance with this meaning. A central theme in the traditional meaning of both holidays is that success or victory was due entirely to God's miraculous intervention on behalf of the Jews and not to any action of the Jews themselves; not even of their leaders. As the traditional *haggadah* (plural *haggadot*) that Jews recite at the inception of Passover states: "And the Lord brought us forth from Egypt, not by means of an angel, not by means of a seraph, nor by means of a messenger: but the Most Holy, blessed be He, Himself, in His glory. . . ." The meaning of Hannukah is conveyed in the prayer that Jews are instructed to repeat three times a day and following every meal during the holiday: "Then didst thou in thine abundant mercy rise up for them in the time of their trouble . . . thou delivered the strong into the hands of the weak, the many into the hands of the few . . . the arrogant into the hands of them that occupied themselves with thy Torah." What, according to the traditional liturgy, did the Jews themselves do? "After this, thy children came into the inner sanctuary of thy house, cleansed thy Temple . . . kindled lights . . . and appointed these eight days of Hannukah." The worldview expressed in such a prayer is hardly reconcilable with a modern movement for national liberation.

The dilemma of reconciling Zionism and the tradition acquires a second dimension in the Jewish-Israeli culture. This is the problem of the relationship between those who settled in the Land of Israel and the Jewish Diaspora, both past and present. Traditional Jewish culture, the Jewish religion, is primarily the product of two thousand years of Diaspora life. It bears the unmistakable imprint of a religious conception of reality and of a people that deemed itself as powerless and homeless in material terms and compensated for this condition in symbolic terms. Zionism sought more than Jewish sovereignty in the Land of Israel and the ingathering of the Diaspora; it called for the redemption of the Jewish people from their own tradition and culture, which Zionists perceived as a product of the unnatural condition under which the Jews had lived for so long. This involved a measure of hostility not only to the Jewish past but to the vast majority of Jewish people living outside the Land of Israel who did not share the Zionist vision of immediate return to the Land of Israel or self-sacrifice on behalf of the establishment of national independence. Exilic Jews were seen as passive, miserable, and oppressed, and the Diaspora, a source of shame and humiliation.

On the other hand, because Zionism claimed to be acting on behalf of the Jewish people and as legitimate successor to the Jewish past, it could never dissociate itself from Diaspora Jewry and Diaspora culture. Israel, its existence as a state and its culture, is meaningful and significant to most Israelis precisely because they perceive it as the great achievement in the struggle of

Jewish history, the culmination of longings embedded in Jewish culture, inseparably linked to the Jewish past and the Jewish people.

In the *yishuv* and the State of Israel, there were, and are, militant Jewish secularists who insist on total separation of Israeli society and culture from any link to traditional Judaism and to Jews outside Israel. At the opposite extreme are the ultrareligious who deny the legitimacy of a so-called Jewish state, which they perceive as the antithesis of authentic Judaism.

However, 94 percent of Israeli Jews (Liebman and Don-Yehiya 1981) affirm the attachment of Israel with Jewish peoplehood, culture, and history. It is among this vast majority of Israeli Jews that one can find those who favor each of the three approaches for reconciling traditional culture and contemporary political needs and values in Israel. Among the 94 percent is a problematic group; the 12 percent who define themselves as religious and are committed to a Jewish state. Even the reinterpretation approach is not quite suitable to them. Their religious orthodoxy precludes their legitimating any transformation or transvaluation. Hence, they really stand outside Israeli civil religion. They evaluate each approach more or less sympathetically but never fully participate in any of them.

In the development of Israeli civil religion we can identify separate periods in which each approach was dominant; although one finds traces of all approaches in every period among different groups. We will associate each approach with the societal goals of the period in which it was dominant and illustrate how traditional symbols were transformed and transvalued in accordance with each approach.

Israeli civil religion has excluded the Arabs (15 percent of the total population). Their traditions (Christian-Arab, Muslim-Arab, Druze, or other) were never deemed relevant in the formulation of Israel's sacred symbols. Efforts to integrate Arabs into Israeli society have been by recognizing and legitimating their minority status with rights to partially autonomous cultures. The Jewish sector has sought to link them economically and politically but not culturally or socially to the larger society (Lustick 1980).

Confrontation and Labor Zionism

As we noted, the confrontation approach is suitable to a culturally sophisticated group deeply rooted in the very tradition whose values it opposes and whose symbols may evoke a negative resonance. Confrontation was the characteristic approach of the Labor Zionist movement, which led the *yishuv* in the two decades preceding the establishment of the state. While other strategies were present in that period, confrontation was the primary mode through which Labor Zionism related to the tradition and by which it developed a symbol system that both reflected and supported its particular values and perceptions of reality.

The Labor Zionist goal included the creation of a new type of Jew and a new society. Its very image of the desirable Jew and desirable society was the mirror image of the traditional Jew and traditional Jewish society. For example, Labor Zionism's attitude toward non-Jews and toward other nations was more universalist than the dominant civil religion of any other period. It deliberately rejected the particularism and ethnocentrism of the Jewish tradition.

Confrontation was reflected in both old and new symbols. Traditional rituals and myths were deliberately inverted in order to accord with new needs and values. Whereas traditional Jews centered the celebration of the holiday of Hannukah around the cruze of oil that miraculously burned for eight days, a popular Hannukah song in the transformation period glorified the modern Zionist pioneers (really the *yishuv* itself) because "we found no cruze of oil, no miracle was performed for us" (Luz 1979).

The Passover celebration begins with a Seder or festive meal at which, as we noted, the *haggadah* is read. The kibbutzim formulated their own *haggadot* (Reich 1972). In general, God was excised; nature, springtime, and nationalist elements were emphasized. Even revolutionary and class struggle themes found expression in the *Haggadot* of the more leftist kibbutzim. A most dramatic expression, however, of the confrontation approach is the statement by Ber Borochov (1881-1917), the foremost ideologue of the Labor Zionist movement. One of the most popular sections of the *haggadah* speaks of four sons: one wise, one wicked, one simple, and one childish. The second son is called wicked because he raises questions about the very basis of the Passover ceremonial and seems to exclude himself from the community of celebrants. Borochov, however, praised the wicked son because that son wanted no part of the freedom given by God but insisted upon attaining freedom by himself. The same "wicked ones," Borochov argued are those who today insist on attaining freedom with their own hands and thereby create "the foundation for the construction of a new Jewish life" (cited in Don-Yehiya and Liebman 1981b).

The strategy of confrontation is applicable to *new* myths and rituals as well. A striking example is the myth of Joseph Trumpeldor (Zerubavel 1980; Don-Yehiya and Liebman, 1981b). The story of Trumpeldor's death and the fall of Tel Hai in 1920 assumed mythic dimensions in the *yishuv* within a year of the event. From the very outset Trumpeldor was projected as an antithesis to the religious tradition, the archetype of the "new Jew" as opposed to the "traditional Jew." Even before his death Trumpeldor had achieved the status of a folk hero, noted for his courage. He was believed to be the first Jew appointed as an officer in the Czarist army. He was the antithesis of the traditional Jew who went to almost any lengths to avoid service in that army.

Comparison between the defenders of Tel Hai and classical Jewish martyrs led Labor Zionist spokesmen to invidious distinctions:

> The early martyrs all sought in return for their deeds . . . a place in the world-to-come—the personal pleasure which every religious Jew feels in giving his life. . . . This was not true of the martyrs of Tel Hai who did not sacrifice their lives for personal pleasure. . . . They were not concerned with whether or not they would earn pleasure in the next world. All that mattered to them was that the Jewish people should survive and the Land of Israel be rebuilt [Hebrew source cited in Don-Yehiya and Liebman 1981b].

According to another Labor Zionist spokesman, unlike Jewish heroes of the past, "Trumpeldor is not merely a victim, a passive hero; he is an active hero." Finally, in what can be described only as the adoption of anti-Semitic stereotypes, Trumpeldor was described as follows: "He had not a trace of sickliness, nervousness, impulsiveness, disquietude—qualities which characterize the Diaspora Jew." Ben-Gurion declared that "for this generation"—those to whom he referred as "the comrades of Trumpeldor"— "this land is more holy than for the tens of generations of Jews who believed in its historical and religious sanctity; for it has been sanctified by our sweat, our work, and our blood" [Hebrew sources cited in Don-Yehiya and Liebman 1981b].

Although the civil religion of Labor Zionism was the most influential system of beliefs and symbols in the prestate period, it did not encompass the entire Jewish community. The religious sector opposed its overt secularism and the Revisionists (ultranationalists) sharply criticized the social component of its belief system.

In a sense, there were several varities of civil religion in the *yishuv* period, each with its own community of believers. The *yishuv* was in fact a federation of relatively voluntaristic and autonomous communities united by their common commitment to the Zionist ideal. Hence, the potential and even necessity for each to develop its own symbol system.

This changed after the establishment of the state. A politically oriented civil religion that strove to unite and integrate the entire Jewish population around the symbolism of the state now emerged. This symbol system called *mamlakhtiut* (statism) was associated with the selectionist approach, although it found its earliest development among the Revisionists in the prestate period (Don-Yehiya and Liebman 1981a).

Selectionism and Statism

Those traditional symbols that pointed to or could be interpreted as pointing to the centrality of the state were integrated into the civil religion; others were ignored. Ben-Gurion and his followers defined and sought to impose their version of civil religion more explicitly than any other group of leaders in any other period. In the years from 1948 to the end of the 1950s Israeli civil religion assumed a political rather than a social orientation, almost meeting the criteria of political religion as Apter (1963) defines it. Apter observes that political religion is particularly attentive to the young in whom it places the hope for the creation of a new generation. It was to this group, a generation removed from firsthand encounter with the Jewish tradition and without the deep associations, memories, and nostalgia of their parents, before whom the statists projected their conception of the tradition.

Ben-Gurion affirmed his unbounded admiration for some aspects of the tradition. On the other hand, he and other statists denied significance to that part of the traditional culture that originated in the period of Jewish exile. They projected the modern settlement of the Land of Israel as the successor to the period of Jewish national independence that ended in 70 C.E. The intervening two thousand years of exile were devoid of meaning.

The result of the exile, according to Ben-Gurion, was to alienate the Jews from their greatest cultural achievement—the Bible. Postbiblical Judaism, he claimed, was apolitical, particularistic, and prone to exaggerated spiritualism. It neither understood nor properly appreciated the Bible and the biblical period with its rich harmony of spiritual and material, moral and political, Jewish and universal teachings. Only those who have returned to their land and lead an independent national life can truly appreciate the Bible (Ben-Gurion 1976:104). While Israel's first prime minister generally refrained from denigrating the rabbinic tradition, the product of the exilic period, his silence with respect to its literature, coupled with his reverence for the Bible and the biblical period was enough. "We are consciously divorcing ourselves from the recent past," he wrote on one occasion (Ben-Gurion 1976:134).

The Bible, in turn, was celebrated not only in the formation of adult study circles, through the major emphasis given it in schools, and in the international Bible quiz that culminated on Israel Independence Day, but in fetishistic veneration as, for example, in the creation of the Shrine of the Book, which housed the Dead Sea Scrolls (Elon 1972:294).

The most important new symbol reflecting the selectionist approach was Independence Day. We have defined selectionism as the affirmation of one strand in the tradition at the expense of others. How can such an approach incorporate new symbols? We argue that one can identify a strategy of selectionism when the new symbol is linked to a traditional one in such a way that one aspect of the tradition is emphasized at the deliberate expense of another.

An association was drawn in the early years of statehood between Independence Day and Passover, an association facilitated by the occurrence of the former celebration thirteen days after the conclusion of the latter festival. There were many references in the first years of statehood to Independence

Day, "that day of days," as a kind of culmination of the process that begins with the Passover celebration of the exodus from Egypt. Independence Day, therefore, replaced Shavuot, the holiday of the giving of the Torah, which was traditionally linked to Passover. The traditional paradigm was exodus (physical freedom) followed by the giving of the Torah (spiritual freedom). The new paradigm became exodus (freedom from foreign oppression by leaving Egypt) followed by Independence Day (achieving national autonomy by establishing the state). The paradigm was strengthened by comparisons between Ben-Gurion and Joshua, who led the Jews into the Promised Land in the biblical period.

Reinterpretation and Israel's New Civil Religion

Neither Labor Zionism and its confrontational approach nor statism and its selectionist approach maintained its dominant position in Israeli political culture. The massive influx of traditionally oriented immigrants following the establishment of Israel was one reason for the decline of the more secular type of civil religions. Indeed, the more secular the civil religion, the greater its difficulty in sanctifying institutions and patterns of behavior because its symbols lack grounding in the collective consciousness and historical culture of the people. The more tenuously the civil religion is linked to the tradition, the more difficult to assert the sacred nature of its myths and rituals. Apter (1963) found this to be true in authoritarian regimes. It is certainly true in a democratic-visionary polity like Israel where the political elite cannot always draw upon the support of state-controlled instruments for socialization in order to maintain the total commitment of the population.

But the need remained for an ideational and symbolic system to legitimate the Jewish state, mobilize internal and external support for its survival and development, and provide content and meaning to its Jewish identity. The reasons behind the decline of Labor Zionist and statist civil religions help account for the rise to dominance of a new civil religion (Liebman and Don-Yehiya 1982) that utilizes the approach of reinterpretation and is more receptive to traditional culture and religion than the other two approaches. The new civil religion reached a dominant position after 1967. The peak of its influence came with the Likud victory in 1977 (the Likud is more closely identified with the new civil religion than any other party), though its roots are to be found in the mid-1950s with the adoption of the Jewish Consciousness Program for Israeli schools. Its goal was to unite and integrate the society around its conception of the Jewish tradition and the Jewish people; it no longer sought the creation of a new Jew and a new Jewish society (Labor Zionism) nor the unification and integration of the society around the symbols of statehood (statism). However, the tradition and Jewish peoplehood, as we shall see, assumed a particular meaning in the new civil religion.

This is the most ethnocentric of all civil religions. It affirms all Jewish his-

tory and culture and gives special emphasis to the isolation of Jews and hostility of Gentiles. The characteristic slogan of this period is the biblical phrase
"a people that dwell alone" or the rabbinic metaphor "Esau hates Jacob." It
is, needless to say, a civil religion especially well suited to masses who are
familiar with and attached to traditional symbols but unsophisticated concerning their explicit meaning.

The tradition is reinterpreted—gently, and unselfconsciously. National
motifs and a nationalist interpretation of religious symbols is omnipresent. For
example, the popular army weekly publication, *In the Camp*, is intended for
the average soldier and the general reader. It also devotes material to each
holiday in the issue immediately preceding the onset of the holiday. In a recent Passover issue the cover reproduced a drawing from an 1849 *haggadah*
showing Moses and the Egyptians at the Red Sea. Of the eight articles, three
related to the holiday. One treated changes in the celebration of Passover in
the kibbutz, stressing that the kibbutzim were now observing more and more
of the traditional rituals. A second analyzed the character of Moses (lonely
and isolated; note the parallel to Israel's contemporary self-image) and observed that "the most magnificent treatment of Moses, the most human and
superhuman of all, and perhaps the most faithful to the truth, is that of the
Torah." (The *haggadah*, it should be observed, never mentions Moses, and
the traditional reason offered is that there is only one hero in the exodus story
and that is God Himself.) The third article recounted the 1920 Arab riots
against Jews in Palestine, noting that they broke out on Passover.

By definition one cannot create a new reinterpreted symbol, but the treatment of the Holocaust illustrates how the strategy of reinterpretation deals
with a symbol of recent origin. Analysis of the Holocaust symbol also provides an instructive comparison of how each of the three approaches deals
with the dilemma of relating the tradition (in this case the tradition of Jewish
suffering and dispersion) to the needs of a modern state.

The Holocaust in Israeli Civil Religion

The very term *Holocaust* (capital H) is a symbol that points to the destruction of European Jewry. It has any number of other meanings and references
according to how it is projected and interpreted. We cannot hope, in so brief
an essay, to explore the problem of the development of the Holocaust symbol
in Israeli society in any depth. Yet the different ways in which the symbol is
projected and interpreted is so dramatic that it lends itself to summary treatment.

As acute an observer of Israeli society as Amos Elon noted that Israelis
"hardly give themselves the chance to forget the Holocaust. The traumatic
memory is part of the rhythm and ritual of public life" (Elon 1972:205-206).
In the words of the army's *Informational Guidelines to the Commander*, the

Holocaust to a great extent fashions "our national consciousness and the way in which we understand ourselves and the world in which we live."[2] In contrast to these observations, it is significant that the mode of observance of Holocaust Day was fixed only in 1959, when the Knesset was called upon to act in the face of widespread public indifference to the day. Until then there were no visible signs of commemoration on Israeli streets; places of entertainment operated as on any other day; there were no special radio programs. Hebrew writers simply ignored the Holocaust during the 1950s. Until the 1960s it found no expression in the school curriculum. It is true that in 1954 the government created Yad Vashem, a public memorial to honor the memory of the Holocaust victims; this today is one of the country's two major shrines. But reading the Knesset debates surrounding its establishment, one senses how problematic the whole matter was to the leaders of Israel. The government acted only under pressure, not the least of which apparently was the fear that memorials would be established abroad that would challenge Israel's status as the legitimate representative of the Jewish people, authorized to speak on behalf of all Jewry, including those who died in the Holocaust.

All this hesitation and reluctance reflected the selectionist approach, which chose to ignore traditional Gentile hostility. According to Ben-Gurion: "German anti-semitism, the Dreyfus trial . . . persecution of Jews in Rumania . . . they represent events from the past in foreign lands, sad memorials of Jews in exile, but not emotional experiences and facts of life which educate and direct us" (Ben-Gurion 1957:8). In other words, this was part of the tradition that the statists refused to incorporate in their symbol system. "The Jewish people erred when it blamed anti-semitism for all the suffering and hardship it underwent in the Diaspora. . . . The cause of our troubles and the anti-semitism of which we complain result from our peculiar status that does not accord with the established framework of the nations of the world. It is not the result of the wickedness or folly of the Gentiles which we call anti-semitism" (Ben-Gurion 1949:12). According to Pinhas Lavon, a member of Ben-Gurion's cabinet and later minister of defense, the Holocaust is not without historical precedent. Jews, he said, were killed in the past. Furthermore, Nazi efforts at genocide had precedent in Turkish attempts to kill all Armenians "and the blood of the Armenian people is no less precious to them than ours is to us" (*Knesset Protocol* 1952:910).

The problem of the Holocaust symbol stemmed in part from the fact that the history of Diaspora Jewry and its condition as a persecuted minority was irrelevant for statists. A second problem stemmed from the Israeli perception of the victims' behavior as one of passivity and surrender—typical of exilic Jewry but one with which Israelis could not identify. Could one acknowledge this without reopening wounds and destroying the unity of the Jews?

The confrontation approach, which we associated with Labor Zionism in the prestate period, faced this challenge squarely. The image of Holocaust victims who went "like sheep to the slaughter" was rife in the *yishuv*. According to one kibbutz *haggadah*: "Hitler alone is not responsible for the death of six million—but all of us and above all the six million. If they knew that the Jew had power, they would not have all been butchered . . ." (Reich 1972:393).

But in the years following the end of the war, overwhelmed by the magnitude of Jewish persecution, by the presence of former concentration camp inmates and European refugees in Israel, and perhaps by their own guilt in having judged the victims so harshly while doing so little to save them, a process of transvaluation began in which the Holocaust symbol now pointed to physical resistance and rebellion. In general it was the political left who remained faithful to Labor Zionist principles and a confrontation strategy whereas the Labor Zionist right wing was attracted to statism and selectionism. The former favored memorializing the Holocaust, and it was they who succeeded in imposing their symbolic model on the commemoration. What they did was to redefine the relevant behavior of the Holocaust victims to coincide with their own values so that the victims became positive rather than negative role models. The day chosen by the Knesset to honor the victims was called Memorial Day for the Holocaust and Ghetto Revolts, and was associated in particular with the Warsaw Ghetto uprising. Yad Vashem's subtitle was Memorial Authority for the Holocaust and Bravery. Knesset members who favored its establishment (they included, we must add, Minister of Education Dinur, in other respects a leading advocate of statism) connected the heroic acts of physical resistance against the Nazis with the heroism of Israeli fighters in the War of Independence.

But the Holocaust is commemorated today in the spirit of the reinterpretation approach. One finds references to bravery and resistence but this is not the major theme. The Holocaust is primarily a paradigm for the condition of Israel and the hostility of its enemies. In the words of the present minister of education, "The Holocaust is not a national insanity that happened once and passed, but an ideology that has not passed from the world and even today the world may condone crimes against us." Contemporary values are, in retrospect, imposed upon the past so that Israelis can derive the meaning they want from the past. The dead, for example, became victims who "sacrificed" their lives purposefully. According to the former president of Israel: "Our decision is firm that the people ingathered again in its ancient homeland will preciously guard these eternal values for which a third of our people sacrificed their life."

Finally the Holocaust symbol points to the debt that the world owes to Israel. According to a Knesset member speaking at the closing ceremony for Holocaust Memorial Day: "Even the best friends of the Jewish people refrained from offering significant saving help of any kind to European Jewry and turned their back on the chimneys of the death camps . . . therefore all the free world, especially in these days, is required to show its repentance . . . by providing diplomatic defensive-economic aid to Israel.''

A Final Word

Our primary concern in this essay has been to illustrate three approaches for coping with the dilemma of tradition and modernity in a new state. We noted, in the case of Israel, that each approach was consistent with a dominant value of the civil religion but we touched upon only the political-economic-social conditions and considerations that give rise to each approach. In addition, whereas the dilemma we have posed is central to the civil religion, there is more to civil religion than the problem to which we have addressed ourselves. There are symbols that point to concerns that have only marginal bearing on the problem. Because the different approaches and strategies are embedded in the civil religion, they are influenced by the general level of public commitment. In this respect, civil religion is quite like traditional religion. We can analyze religion in organizational, ideational, symbolic, or other terms, but we must never overlook the danger of concentrating on its formal properties and ignoring the dimensions of its acceptance or the degree of its penetration or the level of commitment it evokes from its ostensible adherents.

Notes

This article is based on material gathered for the authors' book *Civil Religion in Israel: Traditional Religion and Political Culture in the Jewish State* (Berkeley and Los Angeles: University of California Press, forthcoming). We wish to thank the Israel Foundation Trustees–Ford Foundation for their assistance. This article appeared in *Comparative Politics* (October 1983).

1. Clifford Geertz (1973:238-49) has labeled this the conflict between essentialism and epochalism.
2. Sources in this section, unless otherwise noted, are identified in the original Hebrew in Liebman (1978).

References

Apter, David. 1963. ''Political Religion in the New Nations.'' In *Old Societies and New States*, ed. Clifford Geertz, pp. 57-104. New York: Free Press.
———. 1965. *The Politics of Modernization*. Chicago: University of Chicago Press.
Bellah, Robert. 1980. ''Religion and the Legitimation of the American Republic.'' In *Varieties of Civil Religion*, Robert Bellah and Phillip Hammond, pp. 3-23. New York: Harper and Row.

Ben-Gurion, David. 1949. *In the Conflict*, vol. 4. Tel Aviv: Hotzaat Mapai. (In Hebrew.)

———. 1957. "Concepts and Values." *Hazut*, 3. (In Hebrew.)

———. 1976. *Stars and Dust*. Ramat-Gan, Israel: Massada. (In Hebrew.)

Don-Yehiya, Eliezer, and Charles S. Liebman. 1981a. "Zionist Ultranationalism and Its Attitude toward Religion." *Journal of Church and State* 23 (Spring): 259-73.

———. 1981b. "The Symbol System of Zionist Socialism" *Modern Judaism* 1 (September): 121-48.

Elon, Amos. 1972. *The Israelis*. London: Sphere Books.

Geertz, Clifford. 1973. *The Interpretation of Cultures*. New York: Basic Books.

Knesset Protocol. 1952. Jerusalem.

Liebman, Charles. 1978. "Myth, Tradition and Values in Israeli Society." *Midstream* 24 (January): 44-53.

Liebman, Charles, and Eliezer Don-Yehiya. 1981. "What a Jewish State Means to Israeli Jews." In *Comparative Jewish Politics: Public Life in Israel and the Diaspora*, ed. Sam Lehman-Wilzig and Bernard Susser, pp. 101-9. Ramat-Gan, Israel: Bar-Ilan University Press.

———. 1982. "Traditional Judaism and Civil Religion in Israel." *Jerusalem Quarterly* 23 (April): 57-69.

Lustick, Ian. 1980. *Arabs in the Jewish State*. Austin: University of Texas Press.

Luz, Ehud. 1979. "On the Maccabean Myth of Rebirth." *Hauma* 18 (December): 44-52. (In Hebrew.)

Reich, Avshalom. 1972. "Changes and Developments in the Passover Haggadot of the Kibbutz Movement" Ph.D. dissertation, University of Texas, Austin.

Wilson, John. 1979. *Public Religion in America*. Philadelphia: Temple University Press.

Zerubavel, Yael. 1980. "The Last Stand: On the Transformation of Symbols in Modern Israeli Culture." Ph.D. dissertation, University of Pennsylvania.

4

Gush Emunim: The Institutionalization of a Charismatic, Messianic, Religious-Political Revitalization Movement in Israel

Myron J. Aronoff

Gush Emunim (bloc of the faithful) is both a product of, and an active participant in, helping to shape significant changes in contemporary Israeli political culture. It is a movement that has sought to achieve religious ends through political means, and that has justified extraparliamentary and illegal political actions through the evocation of religious sentiment and authority. To categorize such a movement as either religious or political, or even simply to combine the two terms, inadequately characterizes its complex nature. Even when social scientific concepts, such as charismatic, messianic, and revitalization movements, are employed in the analysis to explain various characteristics of Gush Emunim, these terms must be adapted by emphasizing the unique attributes of the movement, as well as those that it shares with others.

The main analytic focus of analysis is on the process of institutionalization through which Gush Emunim passed from a spontaneous, charismatic, loosely organized, extraparliamentary pressure group on the margins of the political system to a well-organized and functionally differentiated network of related institutions that were incorporated within the present national ruling establishment. To explain the rise and process of transformation of this movement, it is first necessary to sketch briefly the general national, and more specific religious, political, cultural, and subcultural contexts from which it emerged and in which it acted. Against this background—the ideology and

63

worldview, tactics and accomplishments, political support and allies, leadership and organization—the transformation of Gush Emunim will be explored.

This analysis attempts to evaluate the importance of Gush Emunim in effecting as well as reflecting important changes in Israeli society. The case of Gush Emunim is also considered in the context of analogous movements, particularly in the contemporary Middle East.

Background

One of the most distinguishing features of Israeli society is that the major social, economic, and political institutions, and, to a certain extent, aspects of the political culture were self-consciously created by the leaders of the dominant voluntary associations of the Jewish community in Palestine. A newly created society such as Israel faces particularly acute challenges to the taken-for-grantedness of its visionary political culture from the generation succeeding the founders. This is particularly so when the society has undergone dynamic growth and diversification of its population, and of its social, economic, and political institutions. Inevitably disparities arose between changing social realities and the structure of symbolic meanings expressed in the variant versions of the civil religion that were dominant at different stages.[1] Contradictions were exploited for partisan political advantage as well as out of sincere ideological belief. With the corruption of previously "sacred" creeds, attempts were made to revitalize and to reinterpret civil religion in the context of rapidly changing circumstances so as to regain a sense of coherence, meaning, and certainty. This is a study of one such revitalization movement.

The Israeli political system was dominated, both politically and ideologically, by the Labor party (in its various incarnations) for almost fifty years.[2] The political and ideological decline and loss of dominance culminated in the defeat of the party for the first time in the national elections of 1977. The vacuum created by the erosion of the authority of the Labor party, particularly in the last decade prior to its electoral defeat, provided the general context that paved the way for the emergence of Gush Emunim (among other movements). Labor's historic partners in every coalition cabinet, the National Religious party (NRP, also known as Mafdal), provided the more specific political and cultural context that gave birth to the new revitalization movement.

In the period prior to, and shortly after independence, separate school systems were maintained by several of the political movements. When the state educational school system was established, the Histadrut schools were disbanded.

Just as the loss of its independent socialist school system contributed to the undermining of Labor's ideological dominance, the establishment of a separate state religious school system in 1953 under the control of the National

Religious party provided the framework for the development of a subculture from which the Gush Emunim emerged. The leaders, activists, and supporters of Gush Emunim are almost all graduates of the extensive network of institutions of the state religious educational system and related institutions. The new generation of leaders of the National Religious party and of Gush Emunim were trained in high school yeshivot (which combined secular and religious curricula), especially those of B'nei Akiva. As Rubinstein (1982) observed, life in the single-sex religious boarding schools, like that of the agricultural schools of the socialist camp of an earlier period, produced strong social bonds among those who emerged in the 1950s and 1960s as the new national religious elite (cf. Bar-lev 1977).[3] This new generation of national religious leaders, their unity symbolized by the knitted skullcaps they all wear, see themselves as leading a moral renaissance of the entire country.

The founder-leaders of Gush Emunim are all graduates of Yeshivat Merkaz Harav and are the disciples of the late Rabbi Zvi Yehuda Kook, interpreter and exegete of his father, Rabbi Abraham Isaac Kook, the first Ashkenazi chief rabbi of Israel. Having come to the yeshiva to continue their higher religious education after the completion of their army service, they developed close social bonds with one another, and a reverent devotion to their teacher, Rabbi Kook. Rabbi Kook was considered to be naive and unrealistic by the veteran Mafdal leadership. Rubinstein suggests that the fact that Rabbi Kook was the complete opposite of the typical religious party politician may have made him attractive to his idealistic students. Rabbi Kook ascribed to the state mystical and holy authority as precursor of messianic redemption.

Most of the studies of Gush Emunim mention a speech given by Rabbi Kook at a reunion of his former students on Independence Day of 1967. In the midst of his lecture, Rabbi Kook dramatically altered his style of delivery as he told his students how he sat in mourning when the United Nations resolution on the partition of the Land of Israel was announced. He lamented, "Where is our Schem? Where is our Jericho? Where is our Jordan?" Shortly thereafter, as his students participated in what they perceived to be the liberation of these integral parts of the historic Land of Israel, they interpreted their rabbi's speech as having been a case of true prophecy.

The wars of June 1967 and of October 1973 were important milestones in the development of Gush Emunim. Shortly after the 1967 war, a convocation of graduates of Yeshivat Merkaz Harav met and discussed issues related to the newly acquired territories. They decided to establish Yeshivot Hesdare (which combine higher religious studies and military training), which they hoped would be located by the army in the territories to prevent Israeli withdrawal from them. They asked hundreds of rabbis for their interpretation of religious law pertaining to the Land of Israel and whether it was permitted to withdraw from it for any reason. Whereas there were rabbinic opinions that specified conditions under which it was acceptable to return the territories (except Jerusalem) in exchange for peace, Rabbi Kook and those associated with him declared there were no authorized circumstances under which it was acceptable to sacrifice any part of the Holy Land.

The October war of 1973 was called an earthquake in Israel. It was a traumatic event that catalyzed conditions that eventually led to major political changes. National morale was at an all-time low following the war. The unprecedented crisis of confidence in the government led to a proliferation of protest movements and demonstrations that, combined with internal party pressures, led to the resignation of Prime Minister Meir and Defense Minister Dayan (cf. Aronoff 1977). In contrast to the triumphant self-confidence and ecstasy that resulted from the Six-Day War, the post–Yom Kippur War period produced doubt and agony. Gush Emunim was a response to this general social *malaise*, and to the weakness of governmental authority that resulted from this situation, which Gush Emunim both criticized and exploited (cf. Avruch 1978-79).

After a series of preliminary meetings among the founding leaders, Gush Emunim was formally established at Gush Etzion at the end of the winter of 1974. Although originally established as a faction within the NRP, when the parent party joined the government formed by Yitzhak Rabin (after the resignation of Golda Meir) without succeeding in gaining their demand for a government of national unity, including the Likud, Gush Emunim soon severed its official ties with the NRP. However, as I shall discuss shortly, the close symbiotic relationship that remained between Gush Emunim and the NRP was of considerable importance to both groups.

Ideology and Worldview

Although Gush Emunim is characterized by a unique religious political worldview, it has never clearly formulated a comprehensive general ideology. The basis for its worldview can be found in the teachings of Rabbi Abraham Yitzhak Kook as expounded and interpreted by his son, Rabbi Tzvi Yehuda Kook. Further elaborations have been developed by the younger generation of rabbis trained by Rabbi Kook in his yeshiva. Rabbi Kook, the elder, saw in the modern Zionist movement the precursor and harbinger of the messianic process of redemption. The "liberation" of Judea and Samaria was interpreted by Rabbi Kook, the younger, as ushering in the next stage of the process of moral and spiritual redemption. The true believers of Gush Emunim are completely convinced of the historical inevitability of this process (cf. Weissbrod 1982). They firmly believe in the mystical unity of the entire historic Land of Israel and the Jewish people. Given the miraculous liberation of the very heart of the Holy Land, Judea and Samaria, they believe it is the sacred duty of every Jew to inhabit and repossess every portion of the ancestral inheritance. The followers of Gush Emunim related this mystical tie of the people to the Land to the central traditional labor-Zionist value of settlement. In so doing they claim to be the true successors of the pioneering Zionist set-tlement,[4] calling themselves a movement for the renewal of Zionist fulfill-ment. Sprinzak (1981:37) observed: "It is apparent from all its operations and activities that it sees itself as a movement of revival, whose task it is to re-vitalize historic Zionism that died out in the Israel of the fifties and sixties."

> Its complaint is that the state has veered from the self-confident and determined past that marked its earlier success. Instead, it has been overtaken by a lack of resolution and self-doubt. Defined in both secular and religious terms, willing-ness to sacrifice territorial integrity for vague promises of peace is both blunder and moral sin. The consequent policies supported by the movement are an-nexationist bordering on irredentism [Schnall 1979:139].

Rubinstein (1982:126-30) relates how Gush Emunim effectively manipu-lated key symbols of the earlier pioneering era and timed some of its demon-strations to coincide with important nationalistic anniversaries (e.g., the dem-onstration at Sebastia was held on Tel-Hai day). He describes the physical ap-pearance of the Gush Emunim demonstrators, which hearkened back to the veteran pioneers of a previous era: mustachioed men, and women wearing long hair in braids, shirttails out, sweaters tied around the neck, wearing san-dals, knapsacks and weapons hanging at their sides. Many observers of Gush Emunim have commented on its character as a movement of sociopolitical reform and of cultural renewal that confronted an unacceptable reality by nostalgically returning to the sources of what it considered to be good and beautiful in the Jewish and Zionist past. However, none has attempted to analyze it as a revitalization movement, particularly of the messianic variety (cf. Wallace 1956). Janet O'Dea has come closest in her analysis of Gush Emunim as a type of religious sect: but I stress it is more appropriately characterized as a movement.

> The frame of reference in which the issue of the territories is perceived is deter-mined by the deeply rooted prototype of "Jew versus world". . . . They have withdrawn from a world, which in the past oppressed them and in the present would press upon them intolerable compromises. Gush Emunim approaches mundane politics . . . with a "trained incapacity" to disentangle real from sym-bolic. . . . The fierce defensiveness of Gush Emunim is founded upon profound national, social and religious antipathy to the non-Jew, and equally upon fear of the possible unsettling or disintegrative effects of western culture [O'Dea 1976:46].

Given this worldview, it is not difficult to understand the movement's position on relations with the Palestinian Arabs. Although infrequently mentioned in their publications, their position is fairly clear. As Sprinzak (1981:38) succinctly summarized, the Palestinians living in Judea and Samaria should be given the choice: to recognize publicly the legitimacy of Zionism and enjoy full rights as citizens; to obey the laws without recognizing Zionism and enjoy all but political rights; or, with economic incentives, to immigrate to Arab countries.[5]

Gush Emunim's attitude toward democracy, the state, the rule of law, and modern thought are the subject of considerable controversy and disagreement among those who have written on the subject. Sprinzak is the most sanguine about Gush Emunim's respect for the secular institutional expressions of Israeli sovereignty. According to Gush Emunim, democracy is an acceptable system only as long as it remains within a "proper" (as interpreted by Gush Emunim) Zionist framework. Even if a majority of the Knesset was to rule against settlement in Judea and Samaria, by definition this would be an illegitimate act that should be opposed at all costs. Danny Rubinstein and Raanan, both of whom take a more engaged and therefore more polemic stance, express far greater anxiety about the threat that Gush Emunim poses to Israeli democracy.

Tactics

> Ever since its formal founding in the spring of 1974, *Gush Emunim* has been marked by its extra-parliamentary style. The *Gush* was not prepared to confine itself to the framework of the law and the accepted rules of the Israeli political game. From the outset it adopted an extremist style of political action that included demonstrations, protests, unauthorized settlement and the like [Sprinzak 1981:28].

Whereas each of these tactics had been used individually and sporadically by previous groups, Gush Emunim developed them in combination systematically with such effectiveness that some observers conclude that the rules of the political game in Israeli politics have been permanently altered. They became professionals who developed their own political style and special techniques over the years. They adapted their techniques to changing political conditions, the most important of which was the change from Labor governments, which were essentially hostile to their goals, to governments dominated by the sympathetic Likud in 1977. They effectively exploited rivalries within the Labor governments (between Moshe Dayan and Yigal Allon, and between Yitzhak Rabin and Shimon Peres), and received consistent support from the Mafdal ministers. From the beginning they enjoyed easy access to many government ministers, members of the Knesset, and other high-ranking officials of government and other public agencies.[6]

A few weeks after the 1967 war, Kfar Etzion was established west of Hebron, with the government's blessing, at the initiative of a group of predominantly religious settlers, some of whom were members or descendants of members of the original settlement, which had been captured and destroyed during the War of Independence. One of the settlers, Hanon Porat, became one of the most active and visible leaders of Gush Emunim. Another future top leader of Gush Emunim, Rabbi Moshe Levinger, led a group that celebrated Passover in a Hebron hotel in the spring of 1968. A series of events, such as squatting and refusing to leave, negotiations with various cabinet members, and demonstrations, forced the Labor governments first to agree to the establishment of a yeshiva in Hebron (June 1968), and later to allocate 250 housing units (March 1970), which led to the creation of an urban Jewish town (Kiryat Arba) on the outskirts of Hebron, something the government had not intended.

Gush Emunim began its first phase of major protests against the interim agreements with Egypt and Syria in the spring of 1974, reached a peak with several mass rallies, and dwindled after the signing of the agreements. These activities were followed by large demonstrative marches in the territories, usually coinciding with school holidays to ensure a large contingent of religious youths who were free then. Such demonstrations created considerable excitement in religious neighborhoods. The festive atmosphere of the trips to the demonstration sites in Yehuda and Shomron and the national-religious ceremonies and rituals held there created the sense of a continuous party for many of the youthful demonstrators. Even the encounters with the Israeli army, according to Rubinstein, took on the appearance of a game like hide-and-seek that ceased on the Sabbath and was renewed when the Sabbath was over.

The activity for which Gush Emunim is best known is the initiation of settlements across the "green line" (the armistice lines of 1948). The first such settlement established by Gush Emunim in the Golan Heights, Keshet, was actually initiated by members of a kibbutz movement affiliated with the Labor party. Thereafter, Gush Emunim took the initiative in forcing the government to recognize scores of settlements that had been established against the government's wishes. In almost all cases, the government initially agreed to a seemingly modest demand (such as the establishment of a yeshiva in Hebron) that was over time expanded into an urban settlement. The government was similarly pressured into agreeing to the establishment of a camp for workers in the planned industrial zone east of Jerusalem (January 1975), which eventually became the town of Ma'alei Adumim. A similar camp established east of Ramala in March 1975 became the settlement of Ofra. The most dramatic of all was the group led by Benny Katzover and Menachem Felix, which attempted eight times to settle at Sebastia near Nablus, each time being forcibly evacuated by the army. The final confrontation forced the Rabin government to compromise and allow the settlement of Kadum. The same Gush Emunim leaders forced the government to allow the establishment of a "field school," which became the settlement of Elon Moreh.

One of Menachem Begin's first acts before he assumed office after the victory of the Likud in May 1977 was to attend a ceremony in which a Torah scroll (containing the five books of Moses) was placed in the new synagogue at Kadum. He signaled his full support of the settlement efforts of Gush Emunim by declaring (with characteristically dramatic rhetoric) that "we will have many more Elon Morehs." And yet the Likud government continued the previous government's practice of disguising settlements, especially by attaching settlers in military camps, some of which were set up especially for the settlers. The settlement that became Shilo was initially called an "archeological camp."

Rubinstein (1982:74) notes that it was as if the government wanted to establish settlements but was afraid to do so. He claims that the disguised decisions and euphemisms for settlements were signs of weakness that were more self-deceptive than attempts to fool others. This weakness of government, he argues, increased the self-confidence and the missionary feelings of the Gush Emunim settlers. Although this conclusion blurs important differences between the motivations of Labor and the conditions in the Likud governments, the general point is well taken. The internal strains within the Labor governments, particularly that of Yitzhak Rabin, severely weakened them and made them incapable of decisively resolving the conflicting external pressures (particularly from the United States) and internal pressures (from Gush Emunim). To a somewhat lesser extent the same was true for the initial half of the Likud's first term in office. The liberal-moderate forces within the ruling coalition were initially weakened by the split in the Democratic Movement for Change when Professor Amnon Rubinstein led his faction into the opposition. With the resignation of Moshe Dayan (foreign minister) in October of 1979 and Ezer Weizman (defense minister) in May of 1980, and with the former Liberal ministers within the Likud coalition following the hawkish Herut line, the forces of moderation were dealt a mortal blow, and the government thereafter was much more homogeneous. Gush Emunim no longer needed to engage in public demonstrations to accomplish its goals with a government dominated by Begin, Sharon, and Shamir.

However, before this happened, Gush Emunim was dealt a near-fatal blow by Sadat's famous visit to Jerusalem, the dramatic change in national perceptions of the possibility for peace that it precipitated, the Camp David accords, the peace treaty, and the autonomy plan. Gush Emunim failed to mobilize support for demonstrations against Sadat's visit, and the mass support it anticipated in support of its physcial resistance to withdrawal from the town of Yamit in the Sinai failed to materialize (cf. Lewis 1979). The establishment of Atzmona in the northern Sinai in March 1979 in protest against the peace treaty with Egypt was a desperately defiant act of a highly demoralized Gush Emunim. Ironically, it was during this period of greatest demoralization and the low point of public support that Gush Emunim made its most dramatic stride in accomplishing its goal of creating new Jewish settlements in Judea and Samaria, and it did so with the complete cooperation and active support of the government, the army, and the Jewish Agency.

In the ten years of military occupation of the territories, the Labor governments established twenty-four settlements on the West Bank with 3,500 residents mostly in the sparsely populated lower Jordan Valley. Settlements established under the Likud governments in the past five years reflect the goals of Gush Emunim, that is, they are mostly in the heart of the most heavily Arab-populated areas. There are currently around a hundred settlements on the West Bank, with a population of approximately 25,000; on the Golan Heights, thirty-five settlements with 10,000 residents; and in the Gaza Strip, a dozen settlements with 1,000 residents (Rabinovich, 1982:3). Benvenisti estimates that the current budget for development and building on the West Bank is $100 million. Given present rates of annual increase, he estimates that by 1986 there will be a Jewish population of 100,000 on the West Bank (Richardson, 1982).

The settlements have been linked together and to Israel through extensive new networks of highways, and they have also been linked to the Israeli national electric grid and water supplies. The West Bank has also been economically integrated with half the employed labor force working in Israel, more than half of which is employed in construction. This extensive expansion of Jewish settlements on the West Bank was carried out at the initiative of Ariel "Arik" Sharon, who served at the time as minister of agriculture and chairman of the Ministerial Committee on Settlements (who later became minister of defense), and Matityahu Drobles, chairman of the Settlement Department of the World Zionist Organization, with the active support of the military government and an extremely sympathetic chief-of-staff whose views are close to those of Gush Emunim. During the same period Zahal was deployed more extensively on the West Bank.

Citing two critical military orders that laid the legal basis for creating and determining the boundaries of the Jewish regional councils and that established the civilian administration for the territories, Benvenisti convincingly argues that a de facto dual society has been created. "There are two separate systems. One for Jews, now run by Gush Emunim and other settlers, and one for Arabs. . . . The pattern's establishment makes disengagement from the territories more expensive, and the progression is geometric. . . . In the end, disengagement may only come about through trauma or catastrophe'' (Richardson 1982:7). The domestic and regional political implications of these trends are profound.

Political Support: Gush Emunim and Its Allies

Both Raanan (1980:13) and Sprinzak (1981) have called Gush Emunim ''the tip of the iceberg,'' which is based on a much broader sociocultural subsystem in Israeli society. As I mentioned previously, the creation of a separate state religious school system under the control of the National Religious party resulted in the development of a new and distinct subculture in Israeli society, the renaissance of the ''knitted skullcap'' generation. The socioculture environment of these national religious schools, yeshivot, youth movement, and associated institutions led to the emergence of newly synthesized and formulated values that became articulated by the new leaders of the Tze'irim (youths) faction of the NRP and of Gush Emunim. This sociocultural base produced the leaders and activists of both the Tze'irim faction of the NRP and of Gush Emunim, and has remained their most important base of political support (cf. Don-Yehiya 1981).

The nature of the relationship between Gush Emunim and the NRP has been both complex and critical for the success of the former, and in significantly changing the religious as well as political character of the latter. The Tze'irim emerged in the 1960s from a young adult auxiliary of the NRP. It is composed primarily of native-born, urban, middle-class graduates of the aforementioned socialization system, particularly the Bnei Akiva high school yeshivot (cf. Zucker 1973). Having abandoned the kibbutz orientation of the B'nei Akiva youth movement, the faction emphasizes ''the preparation of religious young people to fulfill key positions in the state,'' including the government, the army, and the economy (Schiff 1977:63). Competing for the first time in internal NRP elections in 1968, the Tze'irim received 22 percent of the vote, which led to the entry of the faction's two main leaders, Zevulun Hammer and Dr. Yehuda Ben-Meir, into the Knesset, and eventually into government posts.

Gush Emunim was created by a small homogeneous group of a dozen or so leaders who, in addition to sharing the general characteristics of the new religious elite previously mentioned, graduated during overlapping years from the Yeshivat Merkaz Harav in Jerusalem. They favored efforts within Mafdal to insist that a government of national unity be established that would include the Likud, in order to prevent withdrawal from the occupied territories. In spite of lively debates in the party's central committee, the traditional leadership of the NRP won out and the party joined a coalition with the Labor party. This decision led to the severing of the formal affiliation of Gush Emunim with the NRP. However, the informal relationship that remained was critical in shaping the development of both institutions. Like a rebellious teenager, Gush Emunim criticized and fought with its parent body, and yet continued to receive sustenance from it that enabled it to grow and to develop. Reciprocally, the parent party was reinvigorated by the youthful dynamism and religious-political revival and ideological reformulation that took place through the influence of the Tze'irim and their allies in Gush Emunim. The NRP placed Rabbi Haim Druckman, one of the top leaders of Gush Emunim, in the number-two position on its list of candidates for the Knesset in the 1977 election, and it gained two additional seats there.

The process of secularization, which has particularly affected the Oriental Jewish community in Israel, has contributed to the decline in the NRP's share of the school population from 29 to 24.7 percent between 1968 and 1974. The NRP's long identification with the ruling Labor "establishment" detracted from its public image as well. As Isaac (1981:85) perceptively observed, the territorial issue not only "gave the Mafdal renewed dynamism, it also threatened to split it." The issue has greatly increased ideological tension within the party. The creation of the Techiya (renaissance) party in 1979 by prominent leaders of Gush Emunim and secular ultranationalists (some were from the former Land of Israel Movement and others had left Prime Minister Begin's party in protest against the peace treaty with Egypt) split the Mafdal vote and created serious divisions within Gush Emunim. In the June 1981 election, Techiya received 44,700 votes, which gave it three members in the Knesset, including Hanon Porat of Gush Emunim.

> The absence of unity on an issue held by some religious members to be of central importance suggested that the religious bloc might lose its chief strength—a common definition of the targets of the state. The intrusion of what is simultaneously a secular-national issue into the religious domain has opened the religious parties to the same possibilities for fission and fusion that confront the secular parties [Isaac 1981:85].

Sprinzak correctly stresses that much of Gush Emunim's influence, which has facilitated its achievements, has been based on its political support in the NRP. He argues, "Paradoxically, this also explains why there is little chance that Gush Emunim will become an adventuristic movement" (Sprinzak 1981:45). He argues that because Techiya failed miserably to realize its dream of creating a massive parliamentary opposition block to prevent the ratification of a peace treaty with Egypt, and because NRP funding and support were not as forthcoming to the Gush Emunim after the establishment of Techiya, Gush Emunim members are having second thoughts about their involvement in Techiya.

Recent developments have led to a major rift between Gush Emunim and its most ardent backers in the NRP, Zevulun Hammer and Dr. Yehuda Ben-Meir, the leaders of the Tze'irim. An interview that Hammer, who is minister of education and culture, gave on an evening news program on September 29, 1982, sent shock waves through the Gush Emunim settlements. Hammer indicated that his political thought had been undergoing a change. He expressed regret that the nationalist emphasis on the Land of Israel had overshadowed the religious emphasis on the Torah, which had always been an important part of his party's mission. He expressed his desire to see more balance in the future (cf. Segal 1982:5). Reaction was immediate as several Gush Emunim settlements cancelled visits that Hammer had been scheduled to make—in effect, declaring the minister persona non grata. Others did not cancel his visit but gave him a cool reception, and subjected him to intensive cross-examination about his political positions. Rabbi Haim Drukman, M.K., said he was "astounded and taken back"; and Rabbi Moshe Levinger called on Hammer to resign "in view of his about-turn and treason to the idea of Eretz Yisrael" (Honig 1982:1, 2).

Hammer's close ally, Deputy Foreign Minister Yehuda Ben-Meir, replied to the attacks on Hammer by launching an all-out attack on Gush Emunim. He charged that the Gush "would lead us to eternal war."[7] Although there have been attempts to smooth over differences, some observers feel the rift that has developed is irreversible. There are several explanations for these developments. Through the influence of Gush Emunim and the Tze'irim, the NRP's political policies became practically indistinguishable from those of the Likud, to whom it had lost considerable electoral support. The creation of the ultranationalist Techiya further eroded support for the NRP, particularly among the militants in Gush Emunim. The splitting away of the NRP's young Oriental leader, Aharon Abuhattzeira, who created the ethnic Tami party, further eroded support. Consequently, the NRP lost half of its Knesset seats in the 1981 election. Its leaders are aware of the need to carve a new definitive niche for the NRP in the Israeli political arena. Hammer, in facing the approaching internal party elections, realizes that many of the Gush Emunim activists who had been the mainstay of his support have left the NRP or no longer support his faction. He therefore needs to attract a new party constituency.

Also, the war in Lebanon and its aftermath, including the massacre by Christians of Palestinians who were ostensibly under Israeli protection, has profoundly influenced many religious as well as secular Israelis. Close associates of Hammer claim that he has been particularly influenced by the high casualty rate suffered in the war by soldiers from the Hesder Yeshivot. A crack has appeared in the hawkish views of some of these nationalist religious youth. In television interviews, young Hesder soldiers expressed for the first time the view that it might be worth making territorial sacrifices for peace.

Knitted skullcaps appeared in public protests demanding an investigation of the slaughter of the Palestinians by Lebanese Christian forces in the refugee camps. Rabbis Amital and Aharon Lichtenstein of Har Etzion Yeshiva (among others) brought Jewish ethics to bear in their condemnations of these events. Elhanan Noeh of the Hebrew University observed:

> Yamit was perhaps the first indication that the all-embracing messianism has been undermined. The general religious community was not willing to go to Yamit. . . . Moreover, they were angry with Gush Emunim for pitting Jew against Jew. They weighed it in commonsense, non-messianic terms. I think it was a turning point. The war in Lebanon perhaps continued the process [Furstenberg 1982:9].

For all of these reasons the unique symbiotic relationship between Gush Emunim and the National Religious party, and especially its Tze'irim faction, appears to be coming to an end. Rabbi Haim Drukman no longer represents Gush Emunim in the Knesset on behalf of the NRP. He has recently established an independent faction in the Knesset—Matzad. The loss of the complete and loyal backing of the powerful Tze'irim faction in the party and in the government is likely to considerably weaken the influence of Gush Emunim, and precipitate additional internal realignments within the NRP.

Leadership and Organization

From the beginning the core of top leaders and activists of Gush Emunim remained constant because no provisions were made for electing new leaders. The initial secretariat of nine members, and committee chairmen were in charge of the various spheres of activity. For example, Hanon Porat directed settlement activities, Rabbi Moshe Levinger headed the political department, Yaacov Levine was in charge of finances, and Yehuda Hazani supervised public relations.

The category of spiritual leaders was dominated by the revered teacher, the late Rabbi Zvi Yehuda Kook. Other former teachers such as Rabbi Shlomo Goren (the former chief Ashkenazi rabbi of Israel) and Rabbi Moshe Zvi Neria were also influential. The younger generation of rabbis, Haim Drukman, Moshe Levinger, Eliezer Waldman, Yochanon Fried, and Shlomo Aviner have combined active political roles with their religious and spiritual functions.

In the summer of 1976 Gush Emunim established Amana as its major settlement movement. The establishment of Amana coincided with the decline in the importance of demonstrations and the increasing importance of initiating settlements. Amana became the main institution through which these activities were sponsored, and its full-time paid staff were leaders of Gush Emunim. As settlements were established, they elected secretaries to administer their affairs and representatives to regional councils. For example, Gush Emunim leader Benny Katzover, the original secretary of Elon Moreh, is chairman of the Shomron (Samaria) Regional Council. With the active assistance of the Likud government the number of settlements proliferated, and the regional councils were united under the Council of Jewish Settlements in Judea, Samaria, and Gaza (Yesha), which is chaired by Israel Harel (from Ofra). In the later phase this council has taken on considerable political and administrative responsibility and authority.

There was a heated and divisive debate in Gush Emunim over the proposal to join the new ultranationalist Techiya party. It was decided against aligning Gush Emunim as a group to any parliamentary party, but the members of Gush Emunim were free to join any party they wished. Hanan Porat, who was elected as one of Techiya's three members of the Knesset, and Gershon Shafat were among the prominent Gush Emunim figures that joined Techiya. Rabbi Haim Drukman represented Gush Emunim as a Knesset member for the NRP until recently. Rubinstein reports that most of the central activists joined Techiya, leaving control of Gush Emunim in the hands of secondary echelon leaders, which he claims further lowered its importance as an organization. Others claim that an inner secretariat of approximately six top leaders continues to coordinate Gush Emunim's activities but deliberately avoids publicity.

The routinization, bureaucratization, and diversification of Gush Emunim's activities has led to the specialization of its leaders in different organizational spheres. Some are primarily engaged in settlement activity, others in the administration of the settlements, and others in lobbying and political party activity. Even the two Gush Emunim members of the Knesset represent different political parties (Matzad and Techiya). The main settlement activities are institutionalized through Amana. The Yesha Council carries out some of the political functions, particularly in representing the settlements in dealing with governmental agencies, and the regional councils carry out primarily administrative functions. It appears that Gush Emunim has become incorporated into the main institutional framework of Israeli society. It seems to have been transformed from a militant extraparliamentary antiestablishment political and religious revitalization movement into an institutionally diverse and integral part of the present Israeli political establishment.

There is considerable disagreement, however, in assessing the present status of Gush Emunim:

> There are those, like the spokesman for Kiryat Arba's Rabbi Moshe Levinger, who insist that the Gush no longer exists and that anyone purporting to speak in its name is misleading the public. Others, like the chairman of the Yesha Council . . . Israel Harel, insist that the Gush does still exist in the shape of the settlement movement Amana, and that its political functions have largely devolved

on the Yesha Council. It still remains as an ideological movement, says Harel [Goell 1981:14].

Rubinstein claims that because its organizational power has been transferred to other frameworks, Gush Emunim remains as only a symbol, the crown on the one-time joint activities of a number of different groups (Rubinstein 1982:62). Sprinzak, on the other hand, is convinced that Gush Emunim is alive and well, and continues to be a significant political force for the foreseeable future:

> Both the supporters and detractors of *Gush Emunim* are thus aware that it has become a fact of Israeli political life and that it is there to stay.... *Gush Emunim* has undoubtedly altered the rules of the game in Israeli politics and today it is included among the players... Though extra-parliamentary action was not introduced into Israeli politics by *Gush Emunim*, the *Gush* has greatly increased its role there and will hold the fore for a long time to come [Sprinzak 1981:47].

Militancy Revived: Resistance to Withdrawal from the Sinai

The routinization of the activities of Gush Emunim is not complete, as was apparent in the active leadership role it played in the Movement to Stop Retreat in the Sinai. The Gush Emunim leaders had deep faith that they would bring masses of supporters in sufficient numbers to Yamit to prevent the evacuation, but the masses failed to materialize. The demonstrators attempted to establish "settlements," broke into abandoned homes, and physically obstructed attempts to remove them—staging a dramatic final confrontation with the army on the rooftops, which created considerable public controversy.

Wolfsfeld (forthcoming) points out that because they could not prevent withdrawal, and because serious acts of violence would alienate many of their own supporters as well as the general public, they decided on a policy of "victimization." The idea was to create a national "trauma" to ensure that future settlements on the West Bank, the Golan Heights, and in the Gaza Strip would never be dismantled. He stresses that in spite of pressures to use more extreme measures (especially from Rabbi Meir Kahane's Kach extremists), the level of violence was generally controlled by the leadership to the "threshhold of permissible violence."

The relative restraint shown by Gush Emunim in Yamit may not be shown in the future under different circumstances. First of all, the Sinai does not hold the same intense mystical attachment for the members of Gush Emunim, or for the general religious and/or nationalist public that Judea and Samaria hold. Second, it was clearly in the Likud government's interests as well as Gush Emunim's to make the withdrawal from the Sinai as traumatic as possible (within limits of physical violence) for obvious political reasons. It wanted to show the outside world what a great price it had paid for peace, and it wanted to warn both the American government and Israelis what a calamity there would be if there were to be a withdrawal from the other territories. Perhaps even the apparently senseless act of bulldozing the town of Yamit (which was done ostensibly to prevent its use as a military base) was intended to symbolically and dramatically convey the trauma through the literal destruction of the beautiful town. This explains Gush Emunim's ability to go as far as it did and why it was prevented from going any further.

Analytic Concepts and the Characteristics of Gush Emunim

In his classic essay on the subject, Wallace (1956:265) says: "A revitalization movement is defined as a deliberate, organized, conscious effort by members of a society to construct a more satisfying culture." He particularly stresses that the dissatisfaction with significant aspects of the cultural system, and the conscious effort to initiate broad cultural innovations take the form of reviving what are thought to have been traditional cultural patterns. It is this characteristic of appearing to revitalize values, customs, and symbols of past tradition that gives such movements their name. There are many kinds of revitalization movements. Millenarian movements emphasize supernatural apocalyptic world transformation. Messianic movements emphasize the personification of a divine role in bringing about such world transformation. Charismatic movements revolve around leaders with unique qualities whom the followers consider to have been divinely inspired and/or selected.

Gush Emunim shares characteristics of all of the above types, which it combines to form its own unique corporate persona. It outspokenly rejects many significant aspects not only of modern secular Israeli culture but of religious orthodox positions as well. It rejects modern secular culture for its spiritual barrenness. It condemns the lack of Zionist fervor in the ultraorthodox community and the political pragmatism and lack of vision of the veteran leadership of the national religious community. While drawing from the springs of Jewish mysticism in the Kabalah, its version of messianism and redemption deviates markedly from tradition in its concentration on nationalism and practical politics. As Raanan (1980: ch. 6) points out, the "political theology" of Gush Emunim completely changed the priority of the three pillars of religious Zionist faith—the people of Israel, the Land of Israel, and the Torah of Israel—by stressing the primary importance of the land, or Eretz Yisrael.

Raanan argues that Gush Emunim successfully crystallized around a wide range of frustrations that were felt deeply in many sectors of Israeli society: despair that the "ingathering of the exiles" had not brought more immigrants to Israel's shores; the lack of the realization of the dream of the Greater Land of Israel; despair over the possibility of attaining peace; the continuation of anti-Semitism after the creation of the State of Israel; disappointment due to the gap between the myths of the "new Jew" and the new Israeli society as a "light unto the nations" and reality; and despair with the direction of the development of Israeli society and culture as it was influenced by postindustrial Western culture. Gush Emunim capitalized on the aforementioned despair within a segment of the subculture of the national religious camp—despair among idealistic youths that had become disillusioned with the veteran leadership for what was perceived by the youths to be the failure of the leaders to practice the principles they preached.

Weber's concept of charisma is one of the most widely abused and misapplied concepts in the social science literature. Therefore, it is with considerable care that I apply the term to the spiritual leader of Gush Emunim, the late Rabbi Zvi Yehuda Kook. At first glance he would appear to have been an unlikely candidate to become a charismatic leader, and, in fact, he only became one in the last stage of his long life. Even his former students admit he was barely articulate, and that both his speeches and writings were hard to follow. Yet he clearly cast a spell that created first of all a coterie of devoted disciples, and through them a much larger following. As in similar cases the reciprocal relationship between the charismatic leader and his disciples is critical in explaining the mobilization and expansion of a revitalization movement. When Rabbi Kook died at the age of 92 in 1982, he was mourned by hundreds of thousands who expressed the depth of their grief at his loss. With the death of Rabbi Kook, the process of the institutionalization of charisma, which was already well under way, intensified. The leadership of Gush Emunim became more differentiated, tending to specialize in one of the various spheres of activities carried on through the network of institutional frameworks that the movement had spawned.

Conclusions

Having begun as a movement on the margins of the political system, Gush Emunim has been coopted and incorporated as an integral part of the ruling political establishment in Israel today. It is difficult to evaluate exactly what the impact of the movement has been and is on the political system. Opinions of scholars and politicians are sharply divided. Yitzhak Berman, the Liberal party leader who resigned from the government in protest against Prime Minister Begin's initial reluctance to appoint a judicial commission to investigate the massacre of Palestinians in the refugee camps in Lebanon, claims that "the spirit of Gush Emunim is steadily seizing control of the government, in the military and political spheres alike. The Gush Emunim concept that Israel is alone among the nations is gradually taking root among the government" (*Jerusalem Post*, 1982:3).

The biblical prophecy of Balaam, "Lo, it is a people that shall dwell alone and shall not be reckoned among the nations'' (Num.23:9), according to Labor party Knesset member Rabbi Menachem HaCohen (in a personal conversation with me), was a curse that Gush Emunim has elevated to a blessing. Janet O'Dea (1976:39) claims the aforementioned passage is an expression of ''the prototypical psychological, sociological and theological stance which underlies the movement.'' Yet in their forthcoming study, Liebman and Don-Yehiya argue that this orientation is part of a much broader new civil religion that they claim has gained dominance in Israel in the recent period. Whether this view has gained a dominant position or not may be debatable. However, there is no question that the orientation extends well beyond those identified with Gush Emunim. That this worldview is shared by key members of the present government was vividly expressed by Prime Minister Begin in his letter of August 2, 1982, to President Reagan, in which he compared Beirut to Berlin and Arafat to Hitler.[8] Therefore, it is questionable whether Gush Emunim can be credited or blamed (depending on one's political orientation) with influencing the government. It is more likely that they mutually reinforce a shared worldview.

Similarly, it is difficult to evaluate exactly how influential Gush Emunim has been in getting the present government to implement its settlement policy. Whereas Gush Emunim's influence in pressuring reluctant previous governments, both Labor and the first Likud government, which included Dayan and Weizman, was more clear, the present Likud government appears to be pursuing its own version of settlement. The reserves of idealistic Gush Emunim potential settlers has apparently been nearly depleted. Given the timetable that the government has set itself, it cannot rely on idealism alone to motivate sufficient numbers of people to settle across the green line. The government has therefore engaged in a $150,000 promotion campaign to advertise the financial and other advantages of the new housing it has built and is building, primarily in larger urban concentrations. Given the financial inducements of heavily subsidized apartments, and the fact that many of the new urban areas are close enough to major established urban centers for easy commuting, the number of nonideologically motivated ''settlers'' will soon outnumber their ''pioneering'' predecessors. Gush Emunim's single-minded obsession strengthens the resolve of a government, which is strongly committed to the settlement of Jews in all of the Land of Israel.

Gush Emunim's influence in strengthening the self-confidence of the national religious subculture has been clearly significant. As the most radical expression of nationalist sentiment in the religious camp, it mobilized support for a more militant foreign policy and, through its alliance with the Young Guard of the NRP, played an important role in moving religious Zionism to the forefront of leadership in the most crucial issues facing the nation. Gush Emunim played an active role in moving the religious camp from its defensive posture of self-segregation, which has had profound social, cultural, and political consequences. Even though the leadership of the Tze'irim is moderating its stand, and a new movement of dovish religious Zionists called Netivot Shalom (paths to peace) has arisen as a counterbalance to Gush Emunim's hawkish stand, these phenomena reflect the long-term influence of Gush Emunim in contributing to the new self-confidence of religious Jews in Israel.

Certain aspects of Gush Emunim as a political-religious revitalization movement are comparable to similar movements in the Middle East. The Muslim Brotherhood of Egypt and Syria immediately come to mind as revitalization movements that are religiously based, and that have political goals with far-reaching implications, given their rejection of important aspects of Western "modernity." Likewise, the essays by Green and by Norton in this volume illustrate fascinating cases where in Iran a political-religious movement played a key role in the countermobilization that made possible the successful revolution, and the case in Lebanon where the constraints of the civil war and external factors have thus far prevented the Shia Movement of Hope from realizing its goals.

Political-religious revitalization movements provide serious critiques of contemporary political and cultural systems. They offer dramatic alternative definitions of reality, symbolic systems of cultural meaning, and political agendas that they seek to impose in place of those that are currently dominant. Depending on the nature of the degree of dominance of the regime in power, and the degree to which movements with alternative worldviews are either allowed to participate openly in the political system or are suppressed, as old regimes decline such movements can provide the basis for bringing about substantial reforms or even revolutionary change. It is therefore imperative to keep a close watch on the alternative worldviews presented by groups and movements on the margins of society, for today's marginal groups may become tomorrow's definers of cultural and political realities.

Notes

I am grateful to the Joint Committee on the Near and Middle East of the American Council of Learned Societies and the Social Science Research Council, which awarded me a grant from funds provided by the National Endowment for the Humanities and the Ford Foundation, and to Rutgers—The State University of New Jersey, which awarded me a Faculty Academic Study Program leave and grant that enabled me to conduct research in Israel for a year (1982-83). This essay is the first product of that research. I am also grateful for the helpful comments on an earlier draft of this essay by Professor Kay Lawson, Dr. David Somer, and the members of the Department of Political Science of Tel Aviv University, to whom I presented a seminar based on the early draft.

1. The conceptual framework that informs the analysis of this essay is elaborated by Aronoff (1980, 1982). My discussion of civil religion in Israel appears in Aronoff

(1981b, forthcoming). See Liebman and Don-Yehiya's excellent analyses (this volume, 1981, 1982, forthcoming).
2. For analyses of the Labor party in various historical periods see Shapiro (1976), Medding (1972), and Aronoff (1977, 1979, 1981a, 1983).
3. References to Hebrew sources, especially Rubinstein (1982) and Raanan (1980), are paraphrased rather than translated quotations.
4. Raanan (1980:133-62) elaborates the very substantial differences between the traditional labor-Zionist concept of settlement and that of Gush Emunim.
5. Raanan (1980), A. Rubinstein (1980), D. Rubinstein (1982), Sprinzak (1981), and Weissbrod (1982) give extensive accounts of various aspects of Gush Emunim's ideology.
6. Rubinstein gives detailed accounts of the extensive support received by Gush Emunim. For example, he estimates that approximately 350 families in Kiryat Arba are supported through public funds (D. Rubinstein 1982:81-82).
7. Ben-Meir claims that "the Gush is now advocating that Israel stay on in parts of Lebanon, because these are the lands of the biblical tribes of Naftali and Asher" (Honig 1982:2).
8. The full text of the letter was published in the *Jerusalem Post* on August 4, 1982, p. 8.

References

Aronoff, Myron J. 1977. *Power and Ritual in the Israel Labor Party*. Amsterdam/ Assen: Van Gorcum (Humanities Press).
———. 1979. "The Decline of the Israel Labor Party: Causes and Significance." In *Israel at the Polls: The Knesset Elections of 1977*. Ed. Howard R. Penniman. Washington, D.C.: American Enterprise Institute, pp. 115-45.
———. 1980. "Ideology and Interest: The Dialectics of Politics." In *Political Anthropology*, Vol. 1, *Ideology and Interest: The Dialectics of Politics*. Ed. Myron J. Aronoff. New Brunswick: Transaction, pp. 1-30.
———. 1981a. "Dominant Party Democracy: The Israeli Version." Paper delivered at the annual meeting of the American Political Science Association. New York, September 3-6.
———. 1981b. "Civil Religion in Israel." *Royal Anthropological Institute News* 44:2-6.
———. 1982. "Conceptualizing the Role of Culture in Political Change." In *Political Anthropology*, Vol. 2, *Culture and Political Change*. Ed. Myron J. Aronoff. New Brunswick: Transaction, pp. 1-18.
———. Forthcoming. "The Creation and Corruption of Civil Religion in Israel." In *Power and Complex Organizations*. Ed. F.G. Bailey, Larissa Lomnitz, and Laura Nader. Originally presented at the Burg Wartenstein Symposium No. 84, Burg Wartenstein, Austria, July 19-27, 1980.
———. 1983. "The Labor Party in Opposition." In *Israel in the Begin Era*. Ed. Robert O. Freedman. New York: Praeger.
Avruch, Kevin A. 1978-79. "Gush Emunim: Politics, Religion, and Ideology in Israel." *Middle East Review* 11, no. 2: 26-31.
Bar-Lev, Mordechai. 1977. "The Graduates of the Yeshiva High School in Eretz-

Yisrael: Between Tradition and Innovation.'' Ph.D. dissertation, Bar-Ilan University.

Don-Yehiya, Eliezer. 1981. ''Origins and Development of the *Aguda* and *Mafdal* Parties.'' *Jerusalem Quarterly* 20:49-64.

Furstenberg, Rochelle. 1982. ''Ferment in the Yeshiva.'' *Jerusalem Post*, October 1, p. 9.

Goell, Yosef. 1981. ''Gush Country'' and ''Patriots and Pragmatists,'' *Jerusalem Post International Edition*, February 1-7, pp. 9, 22; and February 15-21, pp. 14-15.

Honig, Sarah. 1982. ''NRP Concerned as Hammer Reveals His Changing Views,'' and ''Gush Emunim Tells Hammer: Don't Visit.'' *Jerusalem Post*, October 1, p. 1; and October 5, p. 2.

Isaac, Real Jean. 1981. *Party and Politics in Israel: Three Visions of a Jewish State*. New York: Longman.

Lewis, Arnold. 1979. ''The Peace Ritual and Israeli Images of Social Order.'' *Journal of Conflict Resolution* 23:685-703.

Liebman, Charles S., and Don-Yehiya, Eliezer. 1981. ''The Symbol System of Zionist-Socialism: An Aspect of Israeli Civil Religion.'' *Modern Judaism* 1:121-48.

———. 1982. ''Israel's Civil Religion.'' *Jerusalem Quarterly* 23:57-69.

———. Forthcoming. *Civil Religion in Israel: Political Culture and Traditional Judaism in the Jewish State*. Berkeley and Los Angeles: University of California Press.

Medding, Peter Y. 1972. *Mapai in Israel*. Cambridge: Cambridge University Press.

O'Dea, Janet. 1976. ''Gush Emunim: Roots and Ambiguities—The Perspective of the Sociology of Religion.'' *Forum* 2, no. 25:39-50.

Raanan, Tzvi. 1980. *Gush Emunim*. Tel Aviv: Sifriat Poalim. (In Hebrew.)

Rabinovich, Abraham. 1982. ''Rate of Settlement to Drop to One per Year, WZO Says.'' *Jerusalem Post*, September 30, p. 3.

Richardson, David. 1982. ''De Facto Dual Society.'' *Jerusalem Post*, September 10, p. 7.

Rubinstein, Amnon. 1980. *Mi Herzl ad Gush Emunim Ubechazera* (From Herzl to Gush Emunim and back). Tel Aviv: Schocken. (In Hebrew.)

Rubinstein, Danny. 1982. *Mi L'Adoni Eli: Gush Emunim* (On the Lord's side: Gush Emunim). Tel Aviv: Sifriat Poalim. (In Hebrew.)

Schiff, Gary S. 1977. *Tradition and Politics: The Religious Parties of Israel*. Detroit, MI: Wayne State University Press.

Schnall, David J. 1979. *Radical Dissent in Contemporary Israeli Politics*. New York: Praeger.

Segal, Mark. 1982. ''Education Minister Zevulin Hammer Talks to Mark Segal about the Aftermath of the Beirut Massacre.'' *Jerusalem Post*, October 15, p. 1.

Shapiro, Yonathan. 1976. *The Formative Years of the Israeli Labor Party: The Organization of Power 1919-1930*. Beverly Hills, CA: Sage.

Sprinzak, Ehud. 1981. Gush Emunim: The Tip of the Iceberg.'' *Jerusalem Quarterly* 21:28-47.

Wallace, Anthony F.C. 1956. ''Revitalization Movements.'' *American Anthropologist* 58:264-81.

Weissbrod, Lilly. 1982. "Gush Emunim Ideology—From Religious Doctrine to Political Action." *Middle Eastern Studies* 18, no. 3:265-75.

Wolfsfeld, Gadi. Forthcoming. "Political Violence and the Mass Media."*Jerusalem Quarterly*.

Zucker, Norman L. 1973. *The Coming Crisis in Israel: Private Faith and Public Policy*. Cambridge: MIT Press.

5

Religion and Countermobilization in the Iranian Revolution

Jerrold D. Green

When viewed in light of other revolutions, the revolution in Iran raises important analytical and conceptual questions. Of a religious character that for the most part was misunderstood, overwhelmingly urban in nature, characterized by the conscious rejection of force by its leadership and following, premised on extraordinarily high levels of popular participation, and achieving success within a remarkably brief time period (one year elapsed from the first major demonstrations to the expulsion of the shah), the Iranian upheaval seems to elude explanation when viewed in terms of conventional theories of revolution. Conceivably, the Iranian case could be considered under the rubric of relative deprivation, a state system under pressure from the international system, or in terms of stages of revolution, yet such notions do not directly address most of the features enumerated above.[1] And although the construction of theory on the basis of one case would be foolhardy, it is still possible to conceptualize events of the Iranian Revolution while modestly contributing to an expansion, not a rewriting, of our understanding of how revolutions come about.

It has been noted that virtually all theories of revolution are concerned with exploring two sets of separate yet interrelated phenomena: (1) the social conditions that lead to revolution; and (2) the character of participation in such revolutions.[2] Various scholars have considered the social and political antecedents to the Iranian upheaval, but few have analyzed the nature of participation in it.[3] Indeed, one of the flaws in the conceptual literature on revolution is its lack of specificity in this regard. Participation in disintegrating politics can be studied just as it can in "healthy" ones. And by attempting to decompose the process of revolution into manageable components, an important incremental process should take hold, for can we understand the whole without taking measure of its parts? Thus, a useful and realistic breakdown of the revolutionary process is suggested. Given that the most difficult to fathom aspect of the Iranian case directly relates both to extraordinarily high levels of participation and to the precise role of religion in stimulating such involvement, the question of participation seems an appropriate starting point for our analysis. Investigation of revolutionary participation should both explain events in Iran and, in a more general sense, suggest an important conceptual variable for the formal study of revolution. Toward this end, this chapter implicitly accepts the argument that revolutions are the products of the very societies they hope to change. Revolutionary participation is inextricably linked to and influenced by participation in the period preceding revolution. And the devastating effectiveness of Iran's oppositional sector can be best understood in terms of a particular type of revolutionary participation that may be termed *countermobilization*.

First used by Walter Dean Burnham in reference to voter realignments in the United States, countermobilization may be simply understood as mass mobilization against a prevailing political order under the leadership of counterelites.[4] Due to its great magnitude, in certain cases such a process can be virtually irreversible. Reliant upon the mobilization capacity of counterelites, the antiregime sector of a society may quickly develop the attributes of a parallel state, rendering a prevailing state structure powerless while itself becoming impervious to attempts to undermine it. It is the process of countermobilization that is the focus of this chapter. Particular attention is paid both to the conditions leading to countermobilization and to its attributes. And while the dynamics of the Iranian case are illuminated by such analysis, Iran also helps to conceptualize the process, yielding a cluster of analytically suggestive indicators of more general applicability.[5]

Mobilization and Political Participation

A classical dilemma afflicting both the governance and the study of the developing areas regards the degree of political participation that a ruling elite should sanction. The most influential advocates of the more liberal approach are Karl Deutsch and Myron Weiner.[6] Deutsch's theory of social mobilization argues that an often unanticipated by-product of the modernization process is politicization. As urbanization grows along with GNP, literacy, exposure to mass media and the vestiges of modernity (e.g., shops, cities, factories), changes from traditional occupations, and so on, it becomes associated with an irreversible desire for political participation. A ruling elite unable or unwilling to recognize such growing politicization is likely to grow out of touch with its populace, and in extreme cases revolution may occur. Myron Weiner agrees with Deutsch, and his notion of a "crisis of participation" attempts to conceptualize the manner in which socially mobilized sectors of a society come into conflict with a ruling elite unwilling to provide opportunities for mass political participation.

Others recognize the potential dangers of social mobilization, although they are less sanguine than Deutsch and Weiner as to the stabilizing potential of relatively unrestricted political participation. Samuel Huntington represents this more skeptical school of thought.[7] Whereas Deutsch fears inadequate political participation, Huntington's concern is with too much. He argues that when participation exceeds institutional capabilities to assimilate it, instability is likely to evolve. Indeed, he asserts that "revolution is the extreme case of the explosion of political participation."[8] In an important assessment of this formulation, however, Charles Tilly criticizes Huntington, noting that "we must disaggregate revolution into its components instead of treating it as a unitary phenomenon. . . ."[9] This highlights a major flaw in Huntington's argument: no distinction between prerevolutionary and revolutionary participation.[10]

David Apter provides a middle ground between Deutsch's advocacy of participation and Huntington's commitment to its restriction.[11] Recognizing the politicizing capabilities of social mobilization *and* the unwillingness of most national elites to respond to it through the expansion of participation, Apter writes of *political mobilization* in which regimes respond to popular desires for participation through attempts to provide its form but not substance. What may be termed *pseudoparticipation* evolves, with an elaborate charade of the participatory process. Sustained by mobilization parties and/or movements, pseudoparticipation attempts to replicate the participatory process without allowing popular input to influence governmental output. Examples of such political mobilization include Egypt's abortive Arab Socialist Union, the Ba'ath Parties of Iraq and Syria, and Iran's Rastakhiz Party (interestingly, Ba'ath and Rastakhiz both mean resurgence). As Binder writes, "it is evident that Apter's mobilization begins where Deutsch leaves off."[12] Thus, where Huntington perceives one solution for the risks of social mobilization, Apter sees another.

Political mobilization, according to Apter, embodies similarities that transcend individual cases. Mobilization systems strive to create a cold war-like atmosphere in which there is a sanctification of political life, an at times charismatic head of state, and the imposition of a political religion managed by a single mobilization party and/or movement. An internal cold war portrays a "modernizing" regime as engaged in an almost holy mission, and noncompliance with its goals is viewed automatically as deviant behavior. There is no middle ground allowed; if one does not actively support the regime, then one is implicitly opposed to it. An example of this ethos may be seen in the shah's introduction of the Rastakhiz party in 1975, where he stated: "Those who [do] not subscribe to [its] principles [are] either traitors, who belong in prison, or nonIranians who [should] be given their passports to go abroad. . . . Each Iranian must declare himself and there [is] no room for fence-sitters."[13] Unsurprisingly, the effectiveness of mobilization regimes is frequently quite limited.[14]

Responses to social mobilization generally take the forms described and/or advocated by Huntington and Apter rather than those of Deutsch. That is, few regimes that have traditionally forbidden participation are likely to take measures assured to decrease rather than increase their control. This was certainly the case in Pahlavi Iran where the shah would periodically attempt either to restrict participation (Huntington) or to replicate the participatory process through pseudoparticipation (Apter). Yet the effects of such tactics served to increase popular hostility among those socially mobilized Iranians eager to have a measure of influence over the manner in which their society was ruled. The Iranian Revolution was preceded by a sustained period of popular opposition to the regime that was an outgrowth of a crisis of participation as described by Deutsch and Weiner.[15] Given the inability of Huntingtonian and Apterian measures to ameliorate this crisis, the Iranian case allows us to investigate the manner in which a crisis of participation may be transformed into revolution, as well as the particular type of revolution that evolved, for all crises of participation do not culminate in revolution. And although Deutsch and Weiner posit a direct relationship between the two, the process by which such transformation is likely to occur has rarely been conceptualized or examined empirically.

From Crisis of Participation to Revolution

Although crises of participation are not uncommon in the developing areas, it must be determined why they so infrequently culminate in revolution. Or, in other terms, we must ask, under what conditions *can* such a crisis lead to national upheaval? Adam Przeworski provides some guidance in this area. Although his concern is with Western industrialized nations, his insights are equally applicable to developing polities, for, as he writes: "Party systems absorb *potentially explosive* political activities and transform them into political participation" (italics added). Furthermore, Przeworski suggests that "when groups cease to play according to the institutionalized rules, alternate forms of political mobilization may emerge: 'parties' become replaced by 'movements.'"[16] Given that Iran had no institutionalized rules by which groups were allowed to play, no *genuine* parties, alternative forms of mobilization did indeed emerge. Thus, the types of restrictions on participation advocated by Huntington did not eliminate desires for participation, nor did pseudoparticipation, as discussed by Apter. Rather, they simply forced potential participants out of the system into what Przeworski calls extrasystemic forms of mobilization. In Iran, the alternate form of mobilization rapidly evolved into countermobilization. Here the role of religion in the Iranian revolution becomes clear as we see a national religious network boasting a high level of popular legitimacy, extensive infrastructural capabilities, and an impressive degree of societal integration able to stimulate and support radical antistate opposition.

Let us for a moment try to establish the basis for the religious sector's successful countermobilization. Iran contains some 80,000 mosques, 1,200 shrines, and 180,000 mullahs.[17] Among these there are roughly 100 ayatollahs, 5,000 hojats-al-Islam, and 11,000 theology students.[18] In Tehran alone, there are more than 5,000 shrine attendants. Ironically, Iranian modernization did not weaken but strengthened the national religious community. For example, the number of religious pilgrims to holy places in Mashad increased tenfold from 332,000 in 1966-67 to 3.5 million in 1976-77.[19] Rises in income, improved transportation, and expansion of the roadway system, all byproducts of Iranian social mobilization, made what was once a long journey into a relatively simple excursion, highlighting the manner in which the infrastructural attributes of Iran's religious sector were strengthened over time and benefited from national modernization.

The linkage between Iran's crisis of participation and its subsequent revolution is not as straightforward as the above discussion indicates. Indeed, there were a variety of intervening factors and events that are considered below. Yet this infrastructural sketch of Iran's religious sector is meant to emphasize the physical attributes that ultimately permitted it, and *only it*, to function as an alternate source of mobilization in the fashion discussed by Przeworski.

Would-be participants were forced out of the system by the shah's unwillingness to expand the scope of genuine political participation. And popular commitment to the religious sector lay in a complex amalgam of genuine reverence for respected religious leaders and/or in a pragmatic attempt to benefit from an organization boasting a unique ability to countermobilize the Iranian masses. Thus, for many, opposition to the shah rather than a commitment to religious values provided the incentive for revolutionary participation.

The Conditions Leading to Countermobilization

To appreciate the antecedents of countermobilization, we should enumerate and apply them to the Iranian case. Obviously, an in-depth analysis of Iran's revolution is not possible within this context. Thus, only particularly illustrative and salient aspects are invoked to flesh out both the conditions leading to *and* the attributes of countermobilization.

The conditions leading to countermobilization are as follows:

(1) The declining coercive will *or* capacity of the state.
(2) A simplification of politics.
(3) Mass polarization.
(4) The politicization of traditionally nonpolitical social sectors.
(5) Crisis-initiating events.
(6) Exacerbating responses by the regime.

The Declining Coercive Will or Capacity of the State

A history of the Iranian Revolution, indeed of Pahlavi Iran itself, provides ample instances of regime-sponsored violence both of an overt military nature and of a more covert sort under the auspices of its widely feared secret police (SAVAK). Yet a more in-depth investigation into the role of state coercion in the periods both preceding and during the revolution is crucial because its broader-gauge appreciation provides a useful perspective into the dramatic success of Iranian countermobilization efforts, for as indicated above, the earliest antecedents to the Iranian Revolution may be traced to a crisis of participation among Iran's most highly socially mobilized sector—the urban middle class. Documentation of this necessitates a brief foray into recent Iranian history.

Prior to the 1975 elections the shah announced his willingness to sanction electoral opposition to the government-controlled Iran-Novin party. In part, this political liberalization was a response to sporadic terrorism as well as to the economic deterioration (e.g., 40 percent inflation, housing shortages) resulting from the ill-conceived doubling of the expenditure level of the fifth Five-Year Plan. Frightened by the ensuing scurry of political activity reflecting popular desires for expanded political participation, the shah backpedaled, put an end to two-party politics, and created a single mobilization party, Hizb-i-Rastakhiz-i-Melli (National Resurgence party). Just as described by Apter, Rastakhiz was meant to generate support for a troubled regime while at the same time simulating the participatory process through pseudoparticipation. Yet Rastakhiz was doomed to failure from the outset. Iranians had seen parties come and go, and greeted the shah's newest attempt to generate support with ambivalence or cynicism.

By 1977 the Rastakhiz party was but a political relic, and popular dissent grew in scope. Highly socially mobilized Iranians were unable to forgive the shah for his abolition of two-party politics. At the same time, the shah was under pressure from President Jimmy Carter, Amnesty International, and the International Commission of Jurists, all critical of Iran's dismal human rights record. Dissident Iranian students staged well-publicized demonstrations in the United States and Western Europe, while Iranians at home were losing patience as the quality of life in the country rapidly and visibly deteriorated. As Tehran was afflicted with extended electricity blackouts throughout the summer of 1977, and the police were engaged in pitched battles with indigent squatters in South Tehran, the Shah spoke loftily of his new campaign to guide Iran toward a "great civilization" and his desire to surpass Sweden by the year 2000![20]

Inspired by the activities of Iranian students abroad, human rights groups, and even the United States government, various middle-class professional and associational groups decided to act. Frustrated by the absence of participatory mechanisms, such groups chose to go outside the system, in the fashion described by Przeworski, to express their dissatisfaction. According to James Bill, "the middle classes in Iran . . . make up over 25 percent of the population."[21] This sector, the one feeling Iran's crisis of participation most keenly, was initially reformist rather than revolutionary in character. It was only later, in coordination with the national religious sector, that opposition groups became sufficiently powerful to seek an end to the Pahlavi dynasty altogether.

Throughout this period, Iran's crisis of participation became most acute, and it is here that the first condition leading to countermobilization, *the declining coercive will or capacity of the state*, is most crucial. This diminished coercive capacity is reminiscent of Theda Skocpol's findings in her analysis of the French, Russian, and Chinese revolutions, where due to "the incapacitation of the central state machineries" a breakdown in the coercive ability of the state resulted.[22] Frequently induced by pressures from the international system, such breakdowns are not unlike that in Iran. Yet rejection of violence by the shah, unlike in Skocpol's cases, was largely self-induced rather than the result of irresistible external or internal pressures. As a result, state-sponsored coercion during the revolution was limited to particular types of situations.

In May of 1977, a group of fifty-three attorneys called for inquiry into the lack of impartiality in the judiciary. In June, the long-banned Writer's Association sent an open letter to the prime minister. Signed by forty of its members, the letter demanded greater cultural freedom and the right to reconstitute the association. Three days later, the National Front sent directly to the shah a similar letter, demanding adherence to the national constitution. The Group for Free Books and Thought was established by publishers seeking the elimination of censorship and severe government restrictions on publishing. A manifesto signed by fifty-six well-known representatives of various groups sought a return to the Constitution, a cessation of human rights violations, abolition of single-party rule, the release of political prisoners, and free elections. Other groups composed of *bazaaris* (merchants), judges, lawyers, teachers, university professors, and students were also active in this period. Mehdi Bazargan, Khomeini's first prime minister, created the Iranian Committee for Freedom and Human Rights. Finally, on the evenings of October 10 through 19, 1977, the Writer's Association sponsored a series of poetry readings at the Goethe Institute in Tehran.[23] The poems, in part, were extremely critical of the current order, and attracted thousands of listeners—an unprecedented liberty in Pahlavi Iran.

Although unanticipated even by their most active participants, the above events heralded the earliest stages of Iran's revolution. And given the shah's historical willingness to employ coercion, often quite brutally, we must ask why such activities were tacitly encouraged through his uncustomary tolerance. In part, the state's acquiescence may be attributed to a modest liberalization—undertaken by the shah in response to international pressure on Iran born of a heightened sensitivity in the West to human rights issues. Other more tangential explanations include the possibility of royal indecisiveness due to the shah's early bouts with cancer and the attendant lassitude resulting from chemotherapy. Additionally, he may have been unwilling to employ coercion so as not to alienate large segments of Iranian society; perhaps recognizing that his tenure would be prematurely curtailed, the shah, conceivably, was attempting to liberalize in order to facilitate the succession to the throne of his son Crown Prince Reza. Given the shah's accession to power at age twenty-three, he was, I suspect, keenly aware of the potential difficulties awaiting his successor.

Although none of the interpretations can be verified with any certainty, it is clear that the liberalization, what some termed the "Tehran Spring," was limited and of short duration. Yet, peculiarly, it did herald a pattern of state behavior in which coercion was used in a limited and particularly inefficient manner, for the shah resorted to coercion in a reflexive rather than preventive fashion, choosing to respond to revolutionary *symptoms* rather than *origins*. There were innumerable instances of the military's repressing assorted processions and demonstrations in which hundreds were killed (e.g., Tabriz, Qum, Jaleh Square), but SAVAK was far less active in this period than usual. And the shah, even after the imposition of total martial law, never tightly clamped down on the most vocal leaders of the revolution, many of whom, unlike Khomeini, were resident in Iran. Preference for highly public military responses alienated most Iranians while providing a series of heroes in whose martyrdom the revolution's legitimacy lay. Popular revolutionary consciousness was raised, and the state never really suppressed the source of opposition to it. Presumably, had the regime put down early middle-class challenges, the revolution would have been forestalled somewhat. But it seems that from the very beginning the shah misread the nature of opposition to him.

On January 7, 1978, the regime went on the offensive, not against its middle-class opponents but instead targeting the most troublesome segment of the religious sector. The Tehran daily newspaper *Etela' at* published a fabricated letter attacking the exiled Ayatollah Khomeini in a vicious and personal fashion. Although historically an opponent of the regime, Khomeini in this period certainly presented no greater threat to regime stability than he had in previous years. Yet curiously the regime unwittingly designated him as the "official" head of a heretofore nonexistent national opposition. The popular response was rioting of unanticipated severity in the holy city of Qum by a citizenry outraged by the regime's attack on a respected religious leader. With these riots a cycle of violent protest began, for forty days later a commemorative gathering was held for those who died earlier. This *arba' een* led to protest, further loss of life, another commemorative after forty days, and so on. With the introduction of the religious sector into the fray and the regime's inability or unwillingness to use coercive means to halt what would soon be of uncontrollable proportions, an important watershed of the Iranian Revolution had been reached.

A Simplification of Politics and Polarization

The primary attribute of countermobilization is its reliance on high levels of popular revolutionary participation. Thus, as a revolutionary form, it is likely to differ from other types of revolution that depend upon armed cadres who, through either coercion or genuine affection, seek popular support over protracted periods of time (e.g., Viet Nam, Cuba, Nicaragua). The case evincing the most superficial similarities to the Iranian experience is that of Algeria. Yet it, too, is markedly different. Although also premised on mass revolutionary participation, the Algerian upheaval was a colonial war of liberation fought against the French while relying heavily on force of arms and terror. Popular support, albeit at high levels, was generated over an extended period by a far more cohesive revolutionary leadership than that in Iran. The key difference distinguishing the two is that, in Iran, Iranian fought Iranian while such astonishingly high levels of participation were achieved so quickly that an indigenous leader was toppled within only one year—a rare achievement in comparison to the lengthy travails of other revolutionary experiences. In large part, this mass participation may be explained by what I have chosen to term the *simplification of politics* and a subsequent *polarization*.

As an antecedent to full-scale countermobilization, a simplification of politics acted to delineate two crude groupings in Iranian society, a not insignificant development in a country of over thirty-five million people. The mechanics of this simplification remain as yet unclear. To attribute it wholly to Iran's oppositional sector grants the opposition greater cohesion, power, and prescience than it deserves; rather, the simplification of politics served as the early stage of polarization, and both are reminiscent of the mobilization system discussed by Apter. Just as national elites in such a system create an internal cold war, forbid fence-sitting, and try to sanctify politics, counterelites can pursue similar goals. At first glance this may seem counterintuitive, and we must ask whether regime opponents are able to employ the same techniques as a political order they oppose yet more effectively. If we remember, however, that revolutions are the products of the very forces they oppose, then such mirror-image emulation, often unwitting, seems plausible. Just as elites in Apter's formulation attempt to reduce politics to its lowest common denominators, counterelites can benefit from doing so. Potential participants are presented with two simple choices, and less dramatic and/or distracting options are simply filtered out. Between what appear to be the forces of light and those of darkness, the popular choice is clear from the outset, and a contest between elite and counterelite legitimacy, charisma, and societal integration can emerge. This was the case in Iran, with Ayatollah Khomeini besting the shah on all counts. Confronted with two highly salient and conflictual poles, and little political life in between them, traditional oppositional elements in Iran flocked to the regime-critical pole. The simplified conflict between the two was highly public, as are most oppositional activities in repressive societies. As the individual poles coagulate, they develop distinct characters, with an oppositional, *positive* pole and an almost repelling *negative* one (the state). When a society rapidly becomes polarized, in part due to a paucity of political options, its regime soon finds itself in direct competition with its critics for popular support. This *competitive mobilization* is in itself a de facto form of official recognition as the state chooses to vie with its competitor rather than to use coercive means to eliminate it. Gradually, the oppositional pole exercises an undiscerning, almost magnetic pull, passively *attracting* supporters rather than actively recruiting them. Importantly, however, influential counterelites provide the positive pole with a rough shape and character while helping to focus and refine grievances against the state. And for every individual formally countermobilized, countless others give in to ephemeral urges to oppose the national political order. In such a competitive situation, the character of counterelites is all important. And given the evident oppositional efficacy, infrastructural attributes, and inherent legitimacy of Iran's religious sector, it soon found itself in an unanticipated and unique oppositional role.

The Qum disturbances in response to the Khomeini letter illustrated to opponents and critics of the shah the mobilization potential of Iran's religious community, for with its introduction into oppositional political activity, the scope and magnitude of what was primarily reformist anti-Pahlavi activity grew dramatically. On January 19 and 20, 1978, the Tehran bazaar closed in response to a joint call for a general strike by Ayatollah Khomeini and Karim Sanjabi of the National Front. Recognizing its inability to generate popular support despite its petitions, letters, manifestoes and poetry readings, Iran's secular middle class adopted a potentially more fruitful stance by pragmatically throwing in its lot with the religious sector. The strike of the Tehran bazaar was the first public instance of cooperation between the two groups, and was illustrative of the countermobilization that would provide the revolution's dynamic.

What were the mechanics of Iran's simplification of politics and polarization? Such events as the Qum disturbances and the strike of Tehran's *bazaaris* brought Iran's incipient revolution within reach of most Iranians, particularly those in the major urban centers. At the same time, the country was flooded with Khomeini's writings as well as taped cassettes of his *khutbehs* (sermons) delivered from his place of exile in Najaf, Iraq. The foreign press avidly followed rising dissent in Iran while the BBC ultimately became an unofficial voice of the revolution. For example, later, when Khomeini moved to the outskirts of Paris, his aides would tell the BBC of a general strike called for the following day. Iranians hearing the BBC would thus learn of Khomeini's call and do as he bid. *Elamiehs* (notices) from the opposition covered the walls of Tehran and other cities, giving Iranians news of the opposition while listing various demands from Khomeini and his aides. Instructions from the ayatollah would be telephoned to Iran, while Xerox machines worked overtime reproducing revolutionary materials. For example, while in Tehran I obtained a recently received communiqué from Khomeini's supporters in Paris. I went to the clerk responsible for photocopying in the government-sponsored research institute where I was based. I quietly called him aside, asked him to make me a copy of it, and he refused. After some insistence on my part, he looked at what I had, derisively said, *""Een copy khoob nist"* (this copy's no good), and extracted a better reproduction of what I wanted from a huge pile on his machine. In and of itself this anecdote seems relatively insignificant. Yet actions such as that by a simple clerical worker, when aggregated throughout Iran, indicate a growing revolutionary force of remarkable durability and power. This man, in his own fashion, was a revolutionary. He was never recruited into a formal oppositional structure but rather responded to stimuli rampant in the Iran of 1978-79. He had two choices: support for the shah or for Khomeini. He, as did most Iranians, chose the latter—giving in to vague although irresistible instincts by supporting what most Iranians were led to believe was good over evil.

The Politicization of Nonpolitical Social Sectors

Given the high levels of popular participation that characterize countermobilization, and that social mobilization affects diverse segments of a society in different ways, we must ask how popular revolutionary consciousness develops. Despite the high levels of social mobilization evident in Iran's urban centers, for example, this process was for the most part restricted to Iran's burgeoning middle class. Thus, according to Farhad Kazemi, such mobilization did not reach deep enough into Iranian society to include the large numbers of peasant migrants who swelled the urban sector.[24] Tehran's population, to illustrate, went from two to four million people between 1966 and 1976, a doubling that resulted from peasants leaving the countryside to seek greater opportunity in the national capital. Although fulfilling some of the criteria for social mobilization (e.g., changes from traditional occupations, exposure to mass media and the vestiges of modernity such as shops, factories, etc.), the migrants, as Kazemi demonstrates, showed little evidence of conventional politicization, such as awareness of their national political leadership, membership in political parties, or voting. Yet the sudden involvement of these migrants in oppositional activities (they were the foot soldiers of the revolution) raises important questions as to their sudden politicization and commitment to oppositional values. Conceptually, such developments highlight the cruciality of distinguishing revolutionary from prerevolutionary participation. And the rapid induction of such *sansculottes* or "shirtless ones" into revolutionary action testifies to the pervasiveness of Iran's simplification of politics and attendant polarization. Simultaneously, the persuasiveness of the national religious sector is emphasized as we begin to understand the manner in which local mullahs were able to involve their constituents in revolutionary action.

Testimony to the rapid politicization of Iran's previously unpoliticized urban masses may be seen in the huge processions of *Tasuah* and *Ashura* where in Tehran alone, over two million people took to the streets in meticulously organized, peaceful marches against the regime. The procession was led by Ayatollah Talegani and Karim Sanjabi of the National Front, the pinnacle of the coalescence of interests discussed earlier. Individual mullahs led their parishioners through the city in separate groups of men and women, leaving no doubt that even the least socially mobilized segments of Iran's urban centers were committed to the revolution. Thus, the incipient revolution itself politicized such people, albeit in a somewhat less sophisticated fashion than the middle classes, and only the stimulus of their mullahs was needed to provide a vehicle for their antistate participation. This process provided countermobilization its form and substance.

Crisis-Initiating Events and Exacerbating Regime Responses

The final antecedent to full-scale countermobilization highlights the dynamic permitting transition from reformism to revolution. In Iran, several events of tremendous national import contributed to increasingly high levels of revolutionary consciousness, for the revolution fed itself, with each triumph leading to greater heights of unity and cohesion.

The first crisis-initiating event and exacerbating regime response was the publication of the falsified Khomeini letter and the subsequent military suppression of demonstrators in Qum. This led to forty-day cycles of demonstrations, military involvement, and violence in which the state provided opportunities for periodic commemorative gatherings as well as an ample supply of martyrs and heroes.

Among other particularly significant crisis-initiating events was the brief military takeover of Tabriz in February of 1978. This led to a purported shake-up of SAVAK and a motion in the Majlis to censure the military for its handling of the incident. A further contributor to the upheaval was the mysterious fire at the Cinema Rex in Abadan in which four hundred perished. Widely believed to be the work of SAVAK, it was perceived as a graphic illustration of the lengths to which the shah would go to discredit his opponents, whom he blamed for the tragedy. The religious sector, acting almost as a parallel state, imperiously opened its own investigation into the origins of the fire, helping to formalize popular views of the religious sector as a natural and legitimate competitor with and successor to the Pahlavi dynasty.

On September 8, 1978—a day to become known as "Black Friday"—serious rioting occurred in Tehran, with hundreds being killed in Jaleh Square. Attempting to capitalize on the tragedy, Khomeini announced that Muslims could not kill other Muslims and thus the troops responsible for the massacre were Israeli. The story was given wide credence in Iran and Black Friday was immediately enshrined in the lore of the revolution, contributing mightily to sentiment in favor of the religious sector and against the state. It also led to martial law in Tehran and in other cities.

Later in September an earthquake struck the small city of Tabas and there were fifteen to twenty thousand deaths. It was widely believed that the religious sector sped aid to the survivors more quickly and efficiently than did the government. This further hardened regime opposition while strengthening the credibility of the religious sector.

On November 4, a large number of students demonstrating at Tehran University were killed by the military; this led to massive rioting. On the following day, rioting continued, several high officials resigned, total martial law was imposed by the shah, and General Azhair was named prime minister.

Finally, the solemn religious month of *Muharram* began, with the overwhelming processions of *Tasuah* and *Ashura*. The religious sector referred to the processions as a referendum against the Shah. This peaceful idiom reflected the tenor of the revolution as a whole.

The regime's exacerbating responses to the crisis-initiating events took consistent forms. Demonstrations were put down with violence, except for *Tasua* and *Ashura*, while other forms of dissent were met with offers of salary increments, lowered taxes, and other financial inducements, as well as with symbolic gestures, such as the closing of gambling casinos or the dismissal of the minister for women's affairs (to mollify the religious community). Yet both the stick and the carrot worked to alienate most segments of Iranian society. While the former tended to emphasize the sacrifices and purity of the oppositionists, the latter served to denigrate it. That is, most regime opponents had little patience with regime attempts to "buy them off." Such cooptative techniques were a time-honored cornerstone of Pahlavi rule and represented for many Iranians what they wanted changed in their society.[25] Additionally, these gestures served to convince the oppositional sector that it was making progress against the state, for otherwise why would the state accede to popular dissatisfaction with such uncharacteristic rapidity and concern?

Countermobilization as a Revolutionary Form

Having discussed the linkage between a crisis of participation and revolution, as well as the preconditions for countermobilization, we should look at the attributes of countermobilization itself. They are as follows:

- Revolutionary participation becomes a common societal norm.
- Oppositional rather than initiative issues are stressed, with an emphasis on negative rather than positive goals.
- Coalition building among diverse and at times conflicting groups is simplified by a diminution in the import of traditionally divisive ethnic, tribal, socioeconomic, generational, educational, religious, and geographic cleavages.
- There is substantial low-level, informal participation rather than high-intensity participation. Countermobilization is reliant on amateur rather than professional revolutionaries.
- Coalitions develop between oppositionists and those in government.
- There is a shifting, amorphous, loosely structured revolutionary leadership with no oppositional center for a regime to crush.
- Due to high levels of popular participation, countermobilization emphasizes nonviolence.
- Mass revolutionary participation is time perishable, dependent upon quick gains, high polarity, and a truncated time-frame.
- Due to unnaturally high levels of unity, countermobilization is likely to culminate in rapid demobilization.

Many of the attributes seem for the most part self-explanatory, given the attention paid above to their preconditions. Yet they should be looked at in order to illustrate the manner in which they relate and contribute to the process of countermobilization as a whole.

Given the increasingly high levels of polarity characterizing Iranian society in 1978-79, and the series of crisis-initiating events that further enhanced this polarity, a situation evolved in which *revolutionary participation became a common societal norm*. This development, enviable from the perspective of any revolutionary, created a situation in which people automatically, reflexly, and uncritically supported anti-Pahlavi groups within their society. This differs from most revolutions in which revolutionary activity is limited or restricted and in which a revolutionary vanguard provides an irreplaceable revolutionary dynamic. An illustration of the degree to which revolutionary sentiments pervaded Iranian society may be seen in a television speech delivered by the shah. Uncharacteristically using "I" rather than the royal "we," he admitted that Iran was in the midst of revolution, and made the startling assertion that he, as an Iranian, supported the revolution.

Given this high level of support for the opposition, recognized even by the shah, we must investigate the factors contributing to it. Several interrelated causes can be forwarded. Of these, one of the most significant is to be found in the behavior of Khomeini and his immediate supporters in which *oppositional rather than initiative issues were stressed, with an emphasis on negative rather than positive goals*. That is, the religious sector tended to portray itself as Iran's most legitimate and potentially effective *antishah* force. Thus, it was viewed as an entity in opposition to something rather than one in favor of something else. And by keeping its character vague and ill-defined, *all* antistate elements could be drawn to it. Whether this was a conscious revolutionary technique or, as is more likely, a consequence of the opposition's inability to keep pace with rapidly changing events, is unclear. Yet the image of Khomeini contained "something for everyone" opposed to the Pahlavi political order. Thus, groups as diverse as the urban middle class, ethnic and religious minorities, and even the left were able to support him due to a crucial, single-goal consensus focused on removal of the shah. Commitment by such groups to Khomeini lay in his ability to countermobilize popular revolutionary participation rather than his being the architect of what at the time was a vaguely defined Islamic Republic.[26] For example, during a strike of the predominantly Arab oil workers in Khuzistan, Khomeini asked them to return to the fields in order to provide for domestic consumption. The workers were unimpressed by the ayatollah's request and returned only after intercession by Mehdi Bazargan, a former director of the National Iranian Oil Company under Mossedegh. Interestingly, it became clear after an interview with Bazargan in Tehran, that he himself was not particularly enamored of Khomeini.[27] Presumably, his skeptical and short-lived commitment to the ayatollah was pragmatic, much like that of many others in Iranian society.

Khomeini's emphasis on his antishah credentials rather than on his goal to create a theocracy in part led to a situation in which coalition building among diverse and at times conflicting groups was simplified by a *diminution in the import of traditionally divisive ethnic, tribal, socioeconomic, generational, educational, religious, and geographic cleavages*. Iran is a multiethnic society in the extreme, with Persians serving as a minority in their own country.

Yet traditional rivalries, such as that between Azerbaijanis and Kurds, which manifested themselves after the revolution, were shelved as all segments of the society worked toward a common goal. This led to some surprising outcomes. For example, over several weeks Tehran was afflicted by nightly blackouts orchestrated by dissident electrical workers. Blackouts were not engineered, however, on Christmas and New Year's Eve out of solidarity with the revolution's Christian participants! Members of Tehran's large and sophisticated intelligentsia quickly supported Khomeini in his goals, their last thought being the creation of a society governed by the mullahs whom they disdained. When the newspapers went out on strike, influential mullahs paid congratulatory visits to newspaper offices while bazaaris collected money to help the striking journalists support themselves. In fact, visceral hatred of the shah fleetingly brought Iran a degree of cooperation and national unity unprecedented in its history and, lamentably, unlikely in its future.

An important aspect of Iranian countermobilization involved the *great development of coalitions between oppositionists and those in government*. This is a common attribute of revolutions, and in Iran took dramatic proportions due to already high levels of countermobilization. Although on the highest levels many such defections have yet come to light, we can cite the case of General Hussein Fardust, former chief of the Imperial Inspectorate, which superseded SAVAK, and a close boyhood friend and classmate of the shah from their days at a Swiss boarding school. Fardust emerged as a postrevolutionary director of SAVAMA, the Islamic Republic's version of SAVAK.

On a somewhat different level, the ouster of the shah was strongly facilitated by the disintegration of the national bureaucracy, most of whose members at middle and lower levels went over to the national opposition. Wildcat strikes paralyzed virtually all segments of the government. Antiregime meetings were held in government offices, and their employees circulated petitions urging individual cabinet ministers to resign. Workers at the Central Bank of Iran provided lists of Iranians who were purportedly taking large amounts of currency out of the country. Government printing presses and Xerox machines churned out antistate materials. Confronted with such internal *and* external pressures, the apparatus of state crumbled within months.

It is difficult to identify an Iranian revolutionary elite with any precision. The most visible leadership was to be found in Ayatollah Khomeini and his circle of advisers in the outskirts of Paris. Yet all of these had important contacts within Iran, and the religious community closed ranks in a rare show of solidarity, for basically the Iranian Revolution boasted a *shifting, amorphous, loosely structured revolutionary leadership with no oppositional center for the regime to crush*. In part, this is attributed to the distance separating Khomeini from his followers in Iran. Yet such an arrangement, which favored the ayatollah's personal security, also embodied severe costs due to the necessity for leadership from afar and long-range communication. Yet within Iran, it would be no exaggeration to argue that countermobilization rendered virtually all of the country's 180,000 mullahs agents of revolution. At the same time, large numbers of bazaaris, professors, teachers, secondary school and university students, lawyers, doctors, urban migrants, and others were actively engaged in attempts to overthrow the shah. Support for the revolution was virtually universal in Iran, and the tide of countermobilization became quickly irreversible because there existed no revolutionary vanguard for the state to suppress. Revolution was everywhere, and its leaders were easily camouflaged by their high level of integration into the society and extraordinary rapid proliferation. With every school, university, and mosque a hotbed of anti-Pahlavism, where could the regime turn to save itself?

Given the extraordinary high level of revolutionary participation, *Iranian countermobilization emphasized nonviolence.* This is not to say that the revolution was nonviolent per se, but rather that the opposition eschewed its employment while the military resorted to coercive tactics in its suppression of various demonstrations, processions, and meetings. The revolutionary sector chose to emphasize idioms of peaceful change that extended to virtually all aspects of the upheaval. The sheer size of the opposition allowed it to oust the shah while generally avoiding armed conflict.

A key attribute of countermobilization is its potentially short life span, for *mass revolutionary participation is time perishable, dependent upon quick gains, high polarity, and a truncated time-frame.* Given such traits of countermobilization as a loosely structured leadership, an unwieldly and cumbersome popular following, its inherent ideological vagueness, and its oppositional, responsive character, the underlying simplification of politics that supports countermobilization cannot last indefinitely, for a society in its throes is like a rudderless ship. Its only link to "normalcy," the primary factor providing cohesion, is its universal opposition to the prevailing political order. People tend not to work during such an upheaval, and food shortages, inflation, and other social ills are exacerbated. Yet on the other hand, because of countermobilization's very nature and magnitude, the rare society able to generate high levels of countermobilization is likely to oust a preeminent ruling elite with unanticipated rapidity.

In light of these considerations, it is not surprising that *due to unnaturally high levels of unity and revolutionary participation, countermobilization is likely to culminate in rapid demobilization,* for once its goal is achieved, disparate social groupings will return to their original niches in a society. Compounding this predictable fragmentation, for the bond among widely differing entities will disappear, is the issue of what shape a postrevolutionary polity will take. Thus, the very factors distinguishing groups will again become salient at a time in which the polity is particularly vulnerable due to the inability of its new ruling elite(s) to consolidate newly found power. Such demobilization was made quite evident in Iran by the intense disagreements within the religious sector as to the desired character of the "new Iran." At the same time, none of Iran's not inconsiderable ethnic minorities were particularly eager to see the institution of a theocracy, instead committing themselves to timeless desires for greater autonomy and cultural freedom. The more liberal middle-class groups were shocked by attendant religious authoritarianism, while even the more traditional middle class, the *bazaaris*, felt threatened by the possible nationalization of enterprises, which would adversely affect their pursuit of business. In the period following the fall of the shah, well-known supporters of the revolution dropped from sight (i.e., Bazargan, Yazdi, Nazih, Ayatollah Shariat-Madari, Bani-Sadr, Ghotbzadeh, Matin-Daftary, Entezzam). And Iranian society was convulsed by futile attempts by the Khomeini regime to exploit unfavorable political developments in order to restore once-high levels of popular mobilization (e.g., the holding of American hostages, the war with Iraq, the blowing up of the headquarters of the Islamic Republican party, assorted assassinations, etc.). Sadly, the very factors that contributed to the early successes of the Iranian Revolution also contributed to its subsequent failures.

Participation and Revolution Reconsidered

The goals of this study have been (a) to suggest serious consideration of political participation as a conceptual variable for the study of revolution, and (b) to clarify the role of religion in stimulating such participation. It has been shown that participation in a prerevolutionary situation or, more precisely, its absence, may lead to national insurrection. Although scholars such as Huntington are technically correct in viewing revolutions as "explosions of participation," they are somewhat too insensitive to the costs of its denial. Popular involvement in the Iranian upheaval was inextricably linked to absences of participation before it even began. It can be argued that a greater awareness on the part of the shah to the politicization accompanying Iranian development might have helped him to preserve his throne. This is Deutsch's major contribution, and his insights have been convincingly verified by the Iranian experience. The most anomalous aspect of Iran's recent history was the complete absence of political participation before the revolution, followed by unprecedently high levels in the revolution itself. Such seeming contradictions are too important to ignore. They can in large part be explained by more than a mere monolithic expression by millions of Iranians; that what was desired was a political order imbued with greater religious orthodoxy. Support for a religious opposition is not necessarily support for religion per se. That is, commitment to Khomeini was, in many cases, as much the product of opposition to the shah as anything else. Certainly, large numbers of Iranians were and still are committed to the ideal of an Islamic political order. But to assume that Khomeini is synonymous with the ideal of an Islamic republic or that such a republic was the goal of *all* Iranians in opposition to the shah would be to simplify and distort the Iranian Revolution to an unacceptable and meaningless degree.

Notes

I would like to thank David F. Gordon, Zvi Gittelman, Daniel Levine, Peter McDonough, and Miroslav Nincic for helpful comments on earlier drafts of this chapter.

1. See, for example, Ted Gurr, *Why Men Rebel* (Princeton: Princeton University Press, 1969); Theda Skocpol, *States and Social Revolutions: A Comparative Analysis of France, Russia and China* (New York: Cambridge University Press, 1979); Crane Brinton, *The Anatomy of Revolution* (New York: Vintage, 1965).
2. Barbara Salert, *Revolutions and Revolutionaries: Four Theories* (New York: Elsevier, 1976), pp. 3-4.
3. Among recent studies devoted to the Iranian Revolution, see, for example, Shahrough Akhavi, *Religion and Politics in Contemporary Iran: Clergy-State Relations in the Pahlavi Period* (Albany: State University of New York Press, 1980); Michael M.J. Fischer, *Iran: From Religious Dispute to Revolution* (Cambridge: Harvard University Press, 1980); Jerrold D. Green, *Revolution in Iran: The Politics of Countermobilization* (New York: Praeger, 1982); Farhad Kazemi, *Poverty and Revolution in Iran: The Migrant Poor, Urban Marginality and Politics* (New York: New York University Press, 1980); Nikki Keddie, *Roots of Revolution: An Interpretive History of Modern Iran* (New Haven: Yale University Press, 1981); Michael Ledeen and William Lewis, *Debacle: The American Failure in Iran* (New York: Knopf, 1981); and Barry Rubin, *Paved with Good Intentions: The American Experience and Iran* (New York: Oxford University Press, 1980).
4. Walter Dean Burnham, *Critical Elections and the Mainsprings of American Politics* (New York: Norton, 1970), pp. 137-38.
5. Cases where this analytical framework might be profitably employed include Poland and the Philippines, each of which seemed to reach the early stages of countermobilization.
6. Karl W. Deutsch, "Social Mobilization and Political Development," *American Political Science Review* (September 1961): 493-507; Myron Weiner, "Political Participation: Crisis of the Political Process," in *Crisis and Sequences in Political Development*, ed. Leonard Binder et al. (Princeton: Princeton University Press, 1971), pp. 159-204.
7. Samuel P. Huntington, *Political Order in Changing Societies* (New Haven: Yale University Press, 1968).
8. Ibid., p. 266.
9. Charles Tilly, "Does Modernization Breed Revolution?" *Comparative Politics* 5 (April 1973): 436-37.

10. This is also the case with subsequent writings; see Samuel P. Huntington and Joan Nelson, *No Easy Choice: Political Participation in Developing Countries* (Cambridge: Harvard University Press, 1976).

11. David Apter, *The Politics of Modernization* (Chicago: University of Chicago Press, 1976).

12. Leonard Binder, *In a Moment of Enthusiasm: Political Power and the Second Stratum in Egypt* (Chicago: University of Chicago Press, 1978), p. 27.

13. Kayhan Research Associates, *Iran Yearbook: 1977/2535* (Tehran: Kayhan Research Associates, 1977), p. 68.

14. See, for example, Aristide Zolberg, *Creating Political Order: The Party-States of West Africa* (Chicago: Rand McNally, 1966); Raymond Hinnebusch, "Political Recruitment and Socialization in Syria: The Case of the Revolutionary Youth Federation," *International Journal of Middle East Studies* 11, no. 2 (April 1980): 143-74.

15. For discussion of Iran's crisis of participation, see my "Psuedoparticipation and Countermobilization: Roots of the Iranian Revolution," *Iranian Studies* 18 (1980): 31-53; and *Revolution in Iran*, chs. 2, 3.

16. Adam Przeworski, "Institutionalization of Voting Patterns, or Is Mobilization the Source of Decay?" *American Political Science Review* 69 (March 1975): 67.

17. Fred Halliday, *Iran: Dictatorship and Development* (New York: Penguin, 1979), p. 19.

18. Ervand Abrahamian, "Structural Causes of the Iranian Revolution," *MERIP Reports* 80 (May 1980): 24.

19. Halliday, *Iran*, p. 19.

20. The great civilization campaign was preceded by a book of the same name, Mohammed Reza Shah Pahlavi, *Bi-su-yi Tammudin-i Buzurg* (Tehran: Sherkat-e Offset-e Sahami-ye Amm, 1978).

21. James Bill, "Iran and the Crisis of 1978," *Foreign Affairs* 57 (Winter 1978-79): 333.

22. Skocpol, *States and Social Revolutions*, pp. 50-51.

23. These poems were subsequently compiled and published; see Naser Mo'azzen, ed., *Dah Shab: Shabha-ye Sha'eran va Nevisandegan dar Anjoman-e Farhangi-ye Iran va Alman* (Tehran: Amir-Kabir, 1978).

24. Kazemi, *Poverty and Revolution in Iran*, pp. 69-70.

25. See Marvin Zonis, *The Political Elite of Iran* (Princeton: Princeton University Press, 1971), pp. 23-25.

26. This vagueness is epitomized by the interpretive conflict currently surrounding the writings of Ali Shari'ati. For an excellent analysis of this conflict, see Ervand Abrahamian, "Ali Shari'ati: Ideologue of the Iranian Revolution," *MERIP Reports* 102 (January 1982): 24-28.

27. Personal interview, Tehran, November 1978.

6

Harakat Amal (The Movement of Hope)

Augustus Richard Norton

This is the first part of an extensive study of the mobilization of Lebanon's Shi'a community, which has long been on the periphery of Lebanon's political system and on the bottom of the country's economic system. Notwithstanding the political activities of individual Shi'a *zu' ama* (political bosses), the Shi'a community *qua* community was marked by quiescence and even irrelevance for the conduct of politics in Lebanon. Only in the late 1960s did incipient efforts to mobilize the community become evident.[1] Those efforts were overtaken by the civil war that began in 1975. While the war temporarily eclipsed the Shi'as' mobilization, it was the war and its broader political and socioeconomic consequences that provided the decisive impetuses for the assertive and important role that the Shi'as are today assuming in Lebanon. (I have corrupted the correct plural form ''Shiya''' so as to render a more readily recognized plural.) Especially in the shadow of the June 1982 Israeli invasion, it is evident that the Shi'as of Lebanon may well play a decisive part in determining the future and perhaps the survival of the Lebanese state.

While population estimates are always chancy in Lebanon—the last official census was conducted fifty years ago—many observers agree that the Shi'as currently constitute the largest single confessional group, representing approximately 30 percent of the population, or from 900,000 to 1,000,000 members.[2] Thus, the Shi'a population now surpasses both the Maronite and Sunni sects that have dominated the Republic since the attainment of self-rule in 1943. The Lebanese confessional system institutionalizes a Maronite presidency, a Sunni premiership, and a Shi'a speakership in the Chamber of Deputies, all by virtue of the respective population shares of the sects established in the 1932 census. Should the Shi'as have the desire and the opportunity to demand the logic of changed demographics, it is clear that a substantial real-location of political power in Lebanon would result. However, for the most part the Shi'as have been occupied by far less grand objectives, in particular the amelioration of their economic deprivation and the rampant insecurity that has characterized *al-Junub,* the South.

Lebanon's Shi'as have long been considered the most disadvantaged confessional group in the country. By most of the conventional measures of socioeconomic status, the Shi'as fare poorly in comparison to their non-Shi'a cohorts. For example, citing 1971 data, Joseph Chamie indicates: the average Shi'a family income was 4,532 Lebanese pounds (£L; 3 £L = $1 in 1971) in comparison to the national average of 6,247 £L; the Shi'as constituted the highest percentage (22 percent) of families earning less than 1,500 £L; the Shi'as were the most poorly educated (50 percent had no schooling versus 30 percent nationwide); and the Shi'a was the least likely, in comparison with other recognized sects, to list his occupation as professional/technical, business/managerial, clerical or crafts/operative and most likely to list it as farming, peddlery, or labor.[3] In his 1968 study, Michael Hudson found that in the two regions where the Shi'as predominate, the Biqa and the South, the percentage of students in the population (about 13 percent) lagged by as much as five percentage points behind the three other regions.[4] Riad B. Tabbarah, analyzing educational differentials, found that in 1971 only 6.6 percent of the Shi'as had at least a secondary education, compared with 15 percent and 17 percent or higher for the Sunnis and Christians, respectively.[5] Citing official Lebanese government statistics for 1974, Hasan Sharif found that while the South had about 20 percent of the national population, it received less than 0.7 percent of the state budget.[6] Sharif's description of the underdevelopment of the South illustrates the conditions under which many Shi'as live.

> The South has the fewest paved roads per person or per acre. Running water is still missing in all villages and towns although water pipes were extended to many areas in the early sixties. Electricity networks were erected at about the same time, but they are inoperative most of the time. Sewage facilities are available only in large towns and cities. Outside the larger centers telephone service is completely absent except for a single manual cabin which is usually out of order. Doctors visit the villages once a week and sometimes only once a month. Clinics are maintained only in large villages and do not function regularly. Hospitals and pharmacies are found only in the larger population centers. Elementary school is usually run in an old unhealthy house provided by the village. Intermediate schools were introduced to the large towns in the mid-sixties.[7]

Based on this writer's own experience in the South from 1980 to 1981, Sharif's description is still essentially correct, except that the conditions described have been exacerbated by eight years of conflict.

A Brief Digression on Social Mobilization and the Shi'as

In an important 1961 article, Karl W. Deutsch elaborated on the concept of "social mobilization."[8] Social mobilization, in effect, has two dimensions: first, it is an indicator of the modernization process (Deutsch cautions that it is not identical with the "process of modernization as a whole");[9] and second, it speaks to the consequences of modernization. As an indicator, the concept subsumes a wide range of variables that when measured over time signal the extent of the changes that are taking place in a given country. Thus, Deutsch counsels that we pay attention to the following clusters of change: exposure to aspects of modern life (e.g., the media, consumer goods, technology); changes in residence, in particular rural to urban migration; occupational changes, for example, shifts from agrarian employment; literacy rates; and changes in income.

The consequences of social mobilization were described by Deutsch as follows:

> In whatever country it occurs, social mobilization brings with it an expansion of the politically relevant strata of the population.

> Social mobilization also brings about a change in the quality of politics by changing the range of human needs that impinge upon the political process. As people are uprooted from their physical and intellectual isolation in their immediate localities, from their old habits and traditions, and often from their old patterns of occupation and places of residence, they experience drastic changes in their needs.[10]

Taking Deutsch's concept as his inspiration, Michael Hudson examined the social mobilization phenomenon in Lebanon and offered persuasive evidence that the country was undergoing rapid, if uneven mobilization.[11]

While under some circumstances the result of the social mobilization process is the emergence of a shared nationality, Deutsch recognized,[12] apropos of Lebanon, that in some settings the social mobilization of the population would lead not to assimilation but to differentiation. The same process may tend to strain or destroy the unity of states whose population is already divided into several groups with different languages or cultures or basic ways of life.[13]

Despite its deprivation, the Shi'a sect was certainly not divorced from the social mobilization process that was under way in Lebanon. Our task, before describing the form that Shi'a assertiveness has taken, is to explain why the Shi'as followed a particular track, and, furthermore, why the rural setting—contrary to theoretical expectations—was seemingly as significant as the urban environment as a locus for political participatory activities[14] by the Shi'as acting as Shi'as.

The most obvious explanation for the Shi'as relative solidarity is the commonplace that it is nearly impossible to escape from one's confessional identity in Lebanon. From the identity card specifying confession to the allocation of privileges along particularist lines, the Lebanese citizen is constantly reminded that he is a hyphenated Lebanese (e.g., Shi'a-Lebanese, Druze-Lebanese, etc.). Not that acute religiosity is particularly widespread, of course, but religious identity defines one's primary social organization, through which political security is maintained.[15] As will be elaborated in a subsequent section, the existent confessional consciousness of the Shi'as was even further enhanced by the widespread feeling that they had suffered the costs of the continuing conflict in Lebanon far more grievously than any other—Lebanese or non-Lebanese—group in the country.

As for the several hundred thousands of Shi'as who settled—permanently or temporarily—in and around Beirut, it is now well acknowledged that such urban residence does not necessarily erase sectarian identities and often has quite the opposite effect.[16] As Hudson remarked, "The crucible of Beirut does not appear to be molding less particularistic Lebanese citizens." "Urbanization appears to fortify, rather than diminish Lebanese parochialism. . . ."[17] Furthermore, even if the urban dweller seeks to cut his village ties, electoral law makes it difficult, even impossible, for him to do so. (The complicated and lengthy legal process involved in an attempt to shift voting rights from one constituency to another effectively forecloses the possibility for most Lebanese.) As Fuad I. Khuri notes, while only 17 percent of Lebanon's population remained rural after the migrations of the fifties, sixties, and seventies, these important demographic shifts remained unrecognized in the electoral law.

> A citizen, irrespective of where he was living or for how long, was required to return to his hometown to exercise the right to vote. Shifting voting rights from one constituency to another is a complicated procedure that requires a court decision. Had the electoral law been amended to give 17% of the parliamentary seats to the rural areas and 83% to the urban areas, the political structure of Lebanon would have been turned upside down. As it was however, the electoral law helped to bind the voter to his village. . . .[18]

Thus, the village followed the villager into the city in both social and political realms; and yet, as argued below, the city is both figuratively and literally close to the village.[19]

As we shall see, the villages of southern Lebanon have been at least as important as Beirut's urban quarters and poverty belt as a spawning ground for the mobilization of the Shi'as. This may be mildly surprising, even taking into account the extraordinary security situation in the South, because some of the fundamental tenets of political development theory assert an important relationship between urbanization and increases in political participation. Before reconciling this apparent divergence, it is pertinent to review briefly some representative statements on the subject of urbanization and participation.

Daniel Lerner, in his treatment of urbanization as the first phase of modernization, argues: "It is the transfer of population from scattered hinterlands to urban centers that stimulates the needs and provides the conditions for 'take off' toward widespread participation."[20]

Karl Deutsch equates, in large part, the very process of change that transforms a society from traditional to modern ways of life with urbanization. Thus, to measure social mobilization, such variables as "changes in residence," "changes from agricultural occupations," and specifically "urbanization" are offered. As a society experiences greater social mobilization (hence urbanization), we are taught to expect an expansion of "the politically relevant strata of the population,"[21] which in turn leads to "increased political participation."[22] Finally, Samuel Huntington makes the point most directly: "Urbanization, increases in literacy, education, and media exposure all give enhanced aspirations and expectations which, if unsatisfied, galvanize individuals and groups into politics."[23]

The object here is not to trivialize the work of others, but to make an important point with respect to Lebanon. The special meaning of urban residence for political participation has been lost in Lebanon, not because of faulty theorizing but because for Lebanon the urban-rural distinction has lost much of its meaning. In a country of 4,015 square miles, a country in which traveling by road to major urban centers from even the most remote villages is possible in three hours and usually much less, a country in which external migration (and return) is a tradition, and in which brutal pulses of violence have propelled cycles of internal migration, the vast preponderance of the population is psychically nonrural.

The pristine village is uncommon, if not rare, in Lebanon. For reasons that are well expounded by Fuad I. Khuri, the isolated village, safe in its customs and traditions, is a vestige of past ethnographies: "Generally speaking, no community (village, suburb, or city) in Lebanon today has physical boundaries corresponding to its sociocultural limits, although this is a matter of degree. What emerges is a phenomenon in which social groups transcend territorial boundaries, a phenomenon more characteristic of suburban than city or village traditions."[24] Khuri's work, published in 1975, is even more relevant in the light of the changes that have taken place in the past eight years.

Thus, in considering the probably overdetermined emergence of the Shi'as described in the remainder of this paper, it should not seem particularly odd that an important locus of mobilization has been the village or that the mobilization followed the pattern of Lebanese confessionalism.

The Imam Musa al-Sadr and the Creation of Harakat Amal

Given the impoverished status of the Shi'as and processes of social mobilization under way in Lebanon, the question in the 1960s was not whether they would take a more aggressive role in Lebanese politics but when and how they would so so. As Michael Hudson noted in his 1968 study, "One of the more interesting political developments in the postwar period has been... the gradual modernization of Shi'a leadership, a trend accompanied, of course, by demands for a greater share of power."[25] Among those contending for the leadership of the Shi'as was a charismatic religious leader, Musa al-Sadr.[26]

Al-Sadr was born in Qum (essentially the religious capital of predominately Shi'a Iran) in 1928, the son of Ayatollah Sadr al-Din Sadr. He was educated in Teheran and received his religious training in a Qum *madrasa* (religious school), one of the several such schools known as Maktab-i-Islam (or School of Islam). He first visited Lebanon (his ancestral home) in 1957, and after receiving an invitation from the Shi'a community of Tyre, relocated in Lebanon in 1959.[27] By a special presidential decree, President Chehab (1958-64) granted him Lebanese nationality,[28] a rare act that was an early confirmation of his growing influence in Lebanon.

By the end of the 1960s, al-Sadr had established himself as the leading Shi'a cleric in the country, a status that was demonstrated when he was named chairman of the newly formed Higher Shi'a Council in 1969, much to the chagrin of his Shi'a political opponents. The council was a direct response by the government to the growing demands of the Shi'as, demands that were loudly voiced by al-Sadr, who had by this time taken the title "Imam."

In 1970, one year after the formation of the Higher Shi'a Council, the imam organized a general strike "to dramatize to the government the plight of the population of southern Lebanon vis-à-vis the Israeli military threat."[29] Shortly thereafter, the government formed a Majlis al-Junub (Council of the South), which was capitalized at £L 30 million and chartered to support the development of the South. Unfortunately, the council soon became more famous for its corruption than its beneficial projects.[30]

With the influx of additional fedayeen in 1970 and 1971, following the conflict in Jordan, the already difficult social and economic problems of the Shi'as were compounded by a rapidly deteriorating security situation. As the pace of fedayeen attacks and Israeli counterattacks stepped up, life in the South became increasingly perilous. With the Lebanese government unable to protect its citizens, al-Sadr made armed struggle one of the motifs of his campaign to mobilize the Shi'as. Following the 1973 October War, he declared that there was "no alternative for us except revolution and weapons."[31] He asserted that "arms are a symbol of manhood,"[32] and at one rally, angrily declared: "From now onwards we're not *metwallis* [a derogatory term for Shi'as sometimes heard in Lebanon]; we are rejectionists; we are avengers; we are a people who revolt against any kind of oppression."[33]

Citing the government failure to provide either security or economic well-being for its Shi'a citizens, the Imam Musa al-Sadr became increasingly vehement and in 1974 founded the Harakat Mahrumeen (Movement of the Deprived). With his new movement, he vowed to struggle relentlessly until the social grievances of the Shi'as (and other deprived Lebanese) were satisfactorily addressed by the government. As Kamal Salibi reports, "He even warned that he would soon have his followers attack and occupy the palaces and mansions of the rich and powerful if the grievances of the poor and oppressed were left unheeded."[34]

Just one year later, al-Sadr's efforts were overcome by the onset of civil war in Lebanon. By July 1975, it became known that a militia adjunct to the Harakat Mahrumeen had been founded.[35] The militia, called Harakat Amal (The Movement of Hope), was trained by al-Fatah and played a minor role in the fighting of 1975 and 1976. Al-Sadr's movement, including the Amal militia, was affiliated with the Lebanese National Movement (LNM) and the fedayeen during the first year of the civil war, but when the Syrians intervened in June 1976 to prevent a defeat of the Maronite-dominated Lebanese Front, al-Sadr split with his allies and staunchly supported the Syrians. The movement's estrangement from the LNM has continued since, as has its close association with Syria.[36] Subsequently, the name Mahrumeen fell into disuse, and the movement that the imam founded came to be known as Harakat Amal (or simply, Amal).

The remainder of this paper deals with Harakat Amal and the important role that it has played in the last few years as a locus for the mobilization of the Shi'as. While Amal has been active in Beirut and the Biqa Valley, as well as the South, the paper dwells heavily on the South. There are three explanations for this narrowing of focus. First, the South has been a symbol for the Shi'as of their suffering and their plight. Second, it is in the South that Harakat Amal has had its greatest significance. Finally, the not inconsiderable difficulties associated with conducting research in Lebanon simply forced this researcher to narrow his horizons.

Impetuses for the Reemergence of Harakat Amal

While Imam Musa's (as he is called by his followers) exertions prior to the civil war certainly were a bellwether of the social mobilization of the Shi'a community, the imam only led a fraction of the politically affiliated Shi'as. Indeed, it was the multiconfessional reform or revolution-oriented parties that

attracted the majority of the politicized Shi'as. The war had made the traditional Shi'a *zu'ama*—political bosses—increasingly irrelevant to politics.
Many young Shi'as joined such groups as the (pro-Syrian) Arab Baath Organization, the Syrian Social Nationalist party, the (Iraq-supported) Arab Liberation Front, or one of the several Communist organizations.[37] Such groups
represented a wide range of grievances and programs, and the only common
denominator among them was their opposition to the Kata'ib-dominated
Lebanese Front and their support for the Palestine Resistance Movement
(PRM). While the motives of Shi'a members may have been ideological or
revolutionary, the fact remains that all of the organizations paid their members, so that the prospect of a salary certainly played at least a part in explaining recruitment. (It is probably impossible to find a Shi'a village or urban
quarter where stories about unemployed youths departing one day and returning a few weeks later sporting a Kalashnikov rifle or a pistol and a wad of
Lebanese lire are not told.)[38]

While al-Sadr's partisans sometimes played consequential roles in the
1975-76 conflict, they were only one group among many that counted a significant Shi'a membership. In fact, the most valuable political currency from
1975 forward was armed strength, and Musa al-Sadr's charisma was no substitute for his inability to field a more substantial military force. Overshadowed by the military might of his many competitors for political influence, and somewhat discredited by his role in the August 1976 fall of the Pal-
estinian-held Shi'a quarter of Beirut, known as Nabaa, to the Kata'ib[39] Sadr,
in effect, retreated to the South with a coterie of dedicated followers. While he
remained active making speeches and strengthening his following in the
South, his national influence from 1976 to 1978 waned significantly. (There
are reports that the imam played an important role during this period in
arousing opposition to the shah among Iran's Shi'as, but the specific nature of
his activities is unknown.)[40]

Three events in the ten-month period from March 1978 to January 1979 ac-
celerated the mobilization of the Shi'a community and contributed to the con-
solidation of Shi'a political influence in a revitalized Harakat Amal. In March
1978 the Israelis launched their first major invasion of Lebanon, Operation
Litani; in August 1978, the Imam Musa al-Sadr disappeared during a still
enigmatic visit to Libya; and, in January 1979, the Islamic Revolution of Iran
toppled the shah. It was these events that, on the one hand, focused the resentment of the Shi'a community on the Palestinians, and, on the other, provided an important myth and exemplar that facilitated the recruitment of
Shi'as to Harakat Amal.

Operation Litani

The Israeli attack, which claimed some one thousand Lebanese lives, mostly Shi'a, and destroyed a significant number of homes throughout the South, not only demonstrated the heavy human price that the Israelis would exact from the residents of the South as a result of the armed Palestinian presence there but also signaled the decisive end of one Israeli security policy—the policy of retribution—and the beginning of another—a policy of disruption. After the 1978 invasion, the Israeli Defense Force (IDF) moved far beyond all but the slimmest pretense of preemption or prevention in its military operations in South Lebanon. Instead, the IDF sought to keep the PRM (and its supporters and sympathizers) constantly on the defensive with relentless air attacks, raids, kidnapping, and house bombings. Up to the ceasefire of July 1981, the disruption campaign was remarkably successful. Palestinian-initiated actions in or from South Lebanon were rare because the fedayeen were almost constantly reacting to Israeli initiatives. The IDF's guiding principle was confirmed by the chief of staff, General Rafael Eytan, when he noted, "We will continue to take action where we want, when we want and how we want. Our own self interest is supreme and will guide us in our actions not to allow terrorists [i.e., fedayeen] to return to the border fence."[41]

A significant consequence of the IDF's offensive was that residents of the South were incessantly reminded that a continuing Palestinian presence in the region would preclude any surcease to the Israeli campaign. Villagers, particularly those living adjacent to the border strip controlled by Israel through Sa'ad Haddad, lived in fear of nighttime raids carried out against those who sympathized with the Palestinians or who were members of Lebanese groups hostile to Israel or Haddad. In a typical raid in December 1980, Israelis and militiamen from the border strip attacked five villages, killing three persons and wounding ten, and damaging or destroying about fourteen houses.[42] Such raids had several important effects. First, persons representing organizations that competed with Harakat Amal for members tended to stay away from their villages and hence from their potential membership. Second, heretofore apolitical villagers learned that the best protection against unwanted early-morning visitors was affiliation with a movement (viz., Amal) that would prevent "undesirables" from entering their villages. Thus, in a number of villages and towns, local residents even established their own security forces, which would patrol during the hours of darkness. Third, there was a clear and widening gulf between the PRM and the villagers of the South. At the same time, similar developments were under way in the Shi'a quarters of Beirut.

By 1980 and 1981, many of even the simplest peasants adopted anti-Palestinian slogans. Rather than the Israelis, it was the Palestinians who were said to be the cause of the villagers' plight. This alienation represented an important, but easily understood, success for the Israeli security apparatus. However, it should be noted that it was the intensity rather than the originality of the villagers' feelings that was remarkable. In fact, the roots of the villagers' disenchantment may be traced to the early 1970s, when Shi'as rallied in support of the Lebanese army after army-fedayeen clashes.[43]

The polarization of the Shi'a and the PRM was also enhanced by the often arrogant, insensitive, and capricious behavior of the fedayeen.[44] Indeed, by the late 1970s it was commonplace when visiting a southern village to hear all manner of vignettes in which the Palestinians were the villains and Lebanese the victims. Thus, the IDF's intensive campaign, beginning in 1978, merely served to enhance the underlying contradictions and tensions that were present even before the Litani Operation.[45]

The Disappearance of the Imam Musa al-Sadr

The Imam Musa al-Sadr, accompanied Shaykh Muhammed Shahadeh Ya'qub and Shafi 'Abas Badr al-Din, arrived in Libya on August 25, 1978, for a visit of unspecified length and purpose. One of the imam's close associates has indicated that the visit was in response to an invitation from the Libyan leader Mu'ammar Qadhdhafi, which al-Sadr accepted so that he could "advocate the return of peace to Lebanon and to work for peace."[46] Prior to arriving in Libya, Sadr had visited Saudi Arabia, Kuwait, and Algeria for the same purposes.

According to a sympathetic account, the imam decided to leave Libya on August 31, 1978, the eve of the Libyan national holiday commemorating the 1970 revolution, after having met with the chief of the Foreign Relations Office, al-Sayed Ahmed al-Shahatey. The Libyans claim that Imam Musa and his colleagues left by air; his followers deny this, and claim that he never left Libya.[47] He has not been heard from since, although occasional reports of dubious origins indicate that he is still alive.[48] Most impartial observers believe him to be dead, as do some of his followers when speaking privately.

Several explanations of the imam's disappearance have been offered but none have been supported by more than conjecture or rumor. It is germane to at least touch upon them because each tells us a bit about Sadr's opponents, if not about the imam himself. According to one version, Qadhdhafi had earlier provided al-Sadr with £L 3 million ($1 million) and the imam could not satisfactorily account for the money, which allegedly ended up in a private bank account in Switzerland; for his malfeasance, Qadhdhafi had al-Sadr murdered or incarcerated. There are several reasons to doubt this report. First, Libyan monies have been distributed to a number of Palestinian and Lebanese organizations (e.g., the Arab Socialist Union) without any semblance of close or even cursory accounting. Second, al-Sadr's closest companions claim that he was deeply in debt ($2 million) when he disappeared, as a result of loans he had signed to support the large technical institute in Burj Ash-Shimali, near Tyre, and that an examination of his personal accounts revealed only very modest sums of cash. Third, al-Sadr's lifestyle was simple, if not ascetic, and there is no reason to believe that he would have hoarded excess cash when he might have used it to support his movement. Finally, al-Sadr's colleagues claim that they told Qadhdhafi that if he could substantiate any fiscal misbehavior on al-Sadr's part, they would gladly agree to the imprisonment or even execution of the imam.[49]

Another version has the shah of Iran employing SAVAK to eliminate the imam. Al-Sadr apparently played at least a minor role in exciting anti-Pahlavi sentiments among Iran's Shi'as. There has traditionally been a very close relationship between Lebanese and Iranian Shi'a religious leaders, particularly because many Lebanese Shi'a *shaykhs* trained in the *madaris* (religious schools) of Iran. Al-Sadr, of course, had studied in Qum. Thus, there is a certain plausibility to this explanation. In fact, when the UN Interim Force in Lebanon (UNIFIL) was formed in March 1978, Iran provided a battalion that was reportedly well staffed with SAVAK agents who kept busy "identifying and isolating followers of the anti-Shah leader Imam Musa al-Sadr."[50] Nonetheless, while the shah had the motive and no doubt the means to eradicate al-Sadr, al-Sadr's followers and the current Iranian regime—both with every incentive to blame the shah—persist in blaming the deed on Qadhdhafi. As an Iranian official noted in 1980, "We consider the Libyan government directly responsible for the mystery that continues to hover over this affair."[51]

While the mystery of al-Sadr's fate remains, his disappearance has been of enormous symbolic importance to Harakat Amal. Al-Sadr has become a national martyr for many Lebanon's Shi'as. By 1979 his face had been added to the panoply of posters that testifies to the multitude of causes and movements in Lebanon. The movement's newspaer, *Amal*, uses a picture of the imam on its masthead and regularly reprints his speeches and comments (usually accompanying them with additional photographs of the imam). From time to time, movement members even identify themselves as "Sadrieen." Most of the younger members of Harakat Amal wear a button or a pendant with al-Sadr's visage on it, and some even sport silk-screened t-shirts depicting him. In a country with precious few heroes, al-Sadr has achieved an especial degree of fame.

Had the imam passed quietly from the scene, it is likely that Shi'a politics in Lebanon would have been far more fractious than it has been for the past four years. While the imam's followers applaud his humanity, selflessness, and staunch commitment to Lebanon's "disinherited" and to Lebanon itself, his detractors point to his tactical shifts of alliances, the witting or unwitting role he played to the benefit of "counterrevolutionary" institutions (viz., the Deuxième Bureau, the Army intelligence bureau) and his political ambitions. Hence, had he continued his efforts in the South, it is unlikely that he would have been able to repair the fissures that divided him from the Shi'a *zu'ama* and their followers and from many of the groups affiliated with the National

Movement. While his disappearance has not eliminated the fissures, it has made them somewhat irrelevant. Many Shi'as have found in the vanished al-Sadr a compelling symbol of their discontent. Al-Sadr's disappearance has complemented and fed a political mood, and has been propitious for the crystallization of the populist Harakat Amal.

The Islamic Revolution

Another factor, of obvious import, has been the success of the Shi'as Iranian coreligionists in deposing the shah. The victory of the Islamic Revolution in January 1979 has been an important exemplar for the Shi'as of Lebanon and an important source of material and political support. One indication of the close relationship between Teheran and the Lebanese Shi'a is the case of Mustafa Chamran. Chamran was the director of the Burj Ash-Shumali Technical Institute until 1979, when he became a member of the Supreme Defense Council in the new Iranian government. (He was reportedly killed in 1981 while visiting the Iraqi front.) It is not illogical to assume that such a well-placed official might have been of immeasurable assistance in securing the help of the Iranian government. While the extent and dimensions of Iran's support are hard to gauge, it is clear that even without more than rhetorical support, the success of the Islamic Revolution has been an important source of pride to Lebanese coreligionists. As we shall see, some Lebanese Shi'a clerics have attempted to mimic their cohorts' success and have taken up a militant role in politics. However, such cases have been episodic, and there is no significant indication that Lebanese Muslims of whatever sect would care to transplant the Islamic Revolution in Lebanon.

The steady organizational growth of Harakat Amal since 1978 is no doubt interesting; however, the fundamental significance of this dynamic movement is to be found not in its structural characteristics but in its social meaning, to which we now turn.

The Meaning of Amal

Harakat Amal is to a large extent the beneficiary of a number of circumstances that it did little to foster. The movement was rescued from obscurity because it offered a culturally authentic identification to Shi'as who had tired of paying the *diya* (blood payment) on behalf of Palestinians, Israelis, and non-Shi'a Lebanese. Nabih Berri's comments on the price paid by the Shi'as are only moderate when compared with what one would hear in the villages of the South in 1980 and 1981 (and one presumes in 1982): "The people of the south, including the Shi'ites have given the Palestinian cause more than all the Arabs combined have given it. They have given the cause their land, their children, their security, their orchards—everything but their honor and dignity.''[52] Thus, the continuing violence in Lebanon established the need for the organization, and as noted in the preceding section, the disappearance of Imam Musa and the victory of Ayatollah Khomeini defined its context. The credit that Harakat Amal's leaders deserve is for capitalizing on a mood—a historical opportunity—and having done so, they filled a vacuum that under differing circumstances might have been filled by the *zu'ama*, an enlightened Lebanese government, or possibly even the Israelis.

We tend to view events through familiar structural prisms, so much of the attention devoted to Harakat Amal has been in the sense that the Shi'as *qua* Shi'as organized themselves in a paramilitary organization that was challenging many of the other paramilitary organizations that have populated the Lebanese scene.[53] For example, in 1980, an otherwise acute, Beirut-based observer of the Lebanese situation summarily dismissed Harakat Amal as just another armed gang among many. But such notions entirely miss the significance of Harakat Amal. As a combatant, the movement has more often than not been overshadowed by its adversaries; even its leaders have been quick to recognize its military weakness: ''If you go by arms, ammunition and equipment, we are probably the weakest party in Lebanon: the smallest organization is probably better armed and better equipped than we are, but our strength lies in our ability to make the people, the masses, carry out our orders, and they do it because they know we are out to meet their demands.''[54] While the comment overstates Amal's weakness, it does highlight the movement's real strength, its capacity for transcending raw military power and, having done so, exerting not insubstanital political influence in Lebanon.

In the South, where Harakat Amal has drawn much of its strength and nurtured its growth, the number of actual members (versus sympathizers) has been incredibly small. In one large village of three to five thousand only ninety persons even held membership cards; in two other important villages only thirty or forty did so. Yet, each of these villages was considered an Amal stronghold. The point is not that the significance of the movement has been exaggerated but that we have to consider the movement in its wider meaning, i.e., as a political statement with which Shi'as affiliated themselves ideationally. In more than a few southern villages, residents identified themselves as Amalists yet had no official connection with the organization.[55] It was quite common to visit a village replete with posters depicting Imam Musa al-Sadr (and the Ayatollah Khomeini), where the *mukhtars*, village notables, and even peasants clearly espoused basic movement mottoes (e.g., ''Lebanon for the Lebanese''; ''If the foreigners leave, the Lebanese can solve their problems'') and to find that Harakat Amal had not one official member there. When the villager said ''I am with Harakat Amal,'' he was confirming that Amal's populist message struck a sympathetic chord. While the movement's leadership might contemplate fundamental restructuring of the Lebanese political system and the role of the Shi'a sect in such a restructured system, the villager's objectives were far less ambitious; in a word, he sought security. Hence the appeal of a movement that called without equivocation for the reestablishment of the legitimate government and its institutions, especially the army; for the support of the Palestinian struggle in Palestine *not* Lebanon; and for the disarming of the militias, thugs, and marauders that have proliferated in all parts of the country.[56]

It was from the villages and towns that Amal drew its strength, and at the same time derived its weakness. Merchants, the agrarian middle class, and overseas Shi'as were important financial supporters of the movement. But, these people did not represent readily mobilizable coercive strength. The wealthy Shi'a citrus growers of the southern coast (south of the Rashidiyye Camp) were especially ardent contributors to the movement; yet beyond an occasional evening meeting, their active participation in movement affairs outside their villages was nil. Dependent as it was on a geographically diverse base of support, of which the basic unit was the village, Harakat Amal was only infrequently capable of concentrating coercive military or political power. Thus, in the South, though perhaps less so in Beirut and the Biqa, the movement was essentially defensive in orientation, certainly through 1981.[57] Harakat Amal was usually at a decided disadvantage when it had to confront its adversaries on their terms.

Arguably, it is not even accurate to speak of one Harakat Amal. In a sense, for every village where Amal sympathies predominated, there was a separate Harakat Amal. The result has been an organization that accurately declared wide support but that often lacked effective control over its members and their activities. Indicative of this lack of control is the following candid comment by an important movement leader: ''Remember that Amal is a movement. Thus, direct orders can often not be given. Instead leadership must be a combination of persuasion, moral example and the like.''

While not lacking in funds or weapons, the movement's infrastructure in the South was very weak as late as 1982. Beset by constant clashes with its Lebanese and Palestinian adversaries, many of its most capable leaders spent the vast preponderance of their time quelling armed clashes and attempting to maintain at least the fiction of a brotherly relationship with the less overtly hostile segments of the Quwat Mustarika (or Joint Forces, which combined PLO and LNM fighters). Organization-building efforts were further stalled by the simple fact that many of the principal leaders continued to pursue their occupations. Physical security was also a major preoccupation because many leaders lived in villages, which while internally secure were located adjacent to military positions manned by the Quwat Mustarika. In one extraordinary case, an important leader in the South lived less than two hundred meters from a military position that apparently had been sited for the express purpose of intimidating and observing him. Harakat Amal was relatively less vulnerable in the Beirut suburbs, especially Ghobierre and Shiyya, where larger concentrations of Shi'as and the self-contained nature of the community facilitated both the growth of the organization and the exclusion of outsiders. (One Ghobierre resident bragged that "fedayeen and leftists do not dare enter.") Hence, in a violence-ridden environment like Lebanon of late, it was the degree of geographical integrity of respective Shi'a populations that largely determined the extent of Harakat Amal's "official" growth.

The result in the South (and possibly in the Biqa as well) was that in the absence of a well-integrated organization, the Harakat Amal label was free for the taking. For many Shi'a villagers, the movement's name was merely a synonym for any collective self-defense activity carried out in the village; this in itself is a persuasive, if imperfect, indicator of the degree to which Harakat Amal had come to be seen as a quintessential Shi'a organization. The Amal name was also adopted, in at least a few cases, by local *shabab* (young bloods) who felt it provided them and their activities a certain legitimacy they would otherwise lack. Furthermore, more than a few Shi'as who had previously belonged to the ALF or any of the several communist organizations, tested the wind and found the time propitious for a change of labels.[58] Indeed, in the spring of 1981, Harakat Amal temporarily suspended its recruitment activities in the South because of the well-founded suspicion that it had recruited quite a few members of questionable loyalty and background.

The characteristics described above are neither surprising or dysfunctional for an emergent communally based organization such as Amal. However, the movement's weak infrastructure had made it vulnerable to cooptation by those who can manipulate the same symbols as Amal, namely the Shi'a clergy. The leadership that replaced Imam Musa is basically secular. While contacts with Shi'a religious leaders are maintained, there is very little evidence of any participation in Amal per se by individual religious shaykhs. While the evidence is incomplete, there are several indications that a minority within the movement would like to see the integration of Amal and the Shi'a clergy.[59] In early 1982, there was reason to believe that the Imam Muhammad Mahdi Shams ad-Din was challenging Nabih Berri for the leadership of the Shi'as, and doing so successfully. While this power struggle seems to have been short-circuited by the Israeli invasion, it can easily be reinitiated.

On the local level, several shykhs who were clearly sympathetic to Harakat Amal's objectives were reluctant to concede a leading role to its secular leaders. Taking the Iranian mullahs as their role models, several of these men took a direct role in organizing village chapters of Harakat Amal replete with militiamen and security activities. One interesting case involved the southern village of Siddiqine, where the local imam was incensed that the ALF had bombed his home. Ignoring movement representatives in the village, he directed and apparently led the village militia. When senior movement officials attempted to bring the shaykh's forces under their control, he thwarted them. It was only after the Imam Muhammad Mahdi Shams ad-Din, at the behest of Amal, convinced the shaykh of Siddiqine to cooperate that he began to do so, and then only grudingly. (Clearly contemptuous of the right of secular officials to represent his constituence, the shaykh remarked, at a meeting attended by the author, "I am Siddiqine and Siddiqine is me.")

Implicit and Explicit Agenda

With the plethora of militias and political groups in Lebanon, there has been a surfeit of political programs complete with prescriptions for curing the country's ills.[60] Before examining Amal's contribution to the crazy quilt of political platitudes and proposals, it is germane to discuss briefly the reasons that it is difficult to present definitively the political program of Harakat Amal, or any other political group for that matter. Most obviously, among the early casualties of any war are the grand ideals for which men believe they fight. The Lebanese Civil War that began in 1975 was different only in that the idealism of the participants faded with astonishing rapidity. While each of the many militias that fought could—to a lesser or greater extent—be connected to some semblance of a political rationale, the (il)logic of the conflict quickly reduced the basis for individual campaigns and clashes to military pragmatism. Indeed, even the tactical rationale for specific clashes was arguable, with a large number of violent incidents sparked by affronts at checkpoints, killings or kidnapping of cohort members or relatives, or the opportunity to loot and rob.[61] War becomes its own justification, and men engaged in it have little time or inclination to reflect on their collective future. Thus, in an environment of near anomie, prescriptions for eradicating the preconditions that engendered the conflict must wait until the combatants exhaust themselves, eliminate each other, or decisive results are otherwise achieved.

The Unacknowledged Agenda

It is important to recognize that Harakat Amal has been acting on two complementary agendas: the first, implicit and publicly unacknowledged by its officials; the second, explicitly enunciated. Before discussing the public agenda, it is appropriate to elaborate upon the hidden agenda. As we have seen, at the local level the primary motive for joining or supporting the movement was—plainly and simply—to find some relief from the rampant lack of security that gripped much of Lebanon. As the increasingly serious and frequent Amal-Quwat Mushtarika clashes of 1981 and 1982 indicated, the primary threat to the Shi'a community's security was perceived to emanate from the *fedayeen* and their supporters in the Lebanese National Movement.[62]

(Literally " self-sacrificers," the term *fedayeen*, essentially denotes Palestinian guerrillas in this context.) Because the presence of Palestinian fighters and their Lebanese allies was seen as an invitation for Israeli attacks, villagers were not surprisingly opposed to the establishment of military positions in their midst. In addition, such positions often resulted in the expropriation of agricultural lands as well as communal and private buildings, and exposed those in the environs to coercion and physcial intimidation. (These unsavory side effects were of course not restricted to locales occupied by the fedayeen, but were merely one symptom of the devolution of coercive power to armed gangs and paramilitary groups throughout Lebanon.)

In effect, the frequent Israeli raids, artillery bombardments, and air strikes dictated the dispersion of opposing forces, and the dispersion of opposing forces fed the resentment and resolve of those who paid the heaviest price. Accordingly, as Harakat Amal gained strength it would further limit the freedom of action of the fedayeen and make the fedayeen more vulnerable to enemy attacks. Thus, the hidden agenda of the movement that aimed at denying the fedayeen access to the Shi'a community could only weaken the fedayeen. The consequences of the growth of Harakat Amal were recognized by both movement officials and leaders of various components of the Quwat Mushtarika. The groups that were most directly threatened by the resurgence of Amal pursued an aggressive campaign to stifle and even eliminate the movement. In particular, the Jabhat Arabiyya, which because of its association with the Bagdad regime of Saddam Hussayn was anathema to the pro-Iranian Amal, and the various Communist factions that were prime competitors for Shi'a recruits, were among the most militant.

While Fatah officials recognized the threat represented by a strong Amal, they also recognized the imperative for maintaining at least the appearance of good relations with the Shi'a community. Hence, Fatah strove to avoid any open hostility to the movement. For their part, Amal officials were quick to express their distrust of Fatah, which they believed at least sought to contain their movement, but they also recognized the utility of Fatah as a *wasita* (mediator). It should be emphasized that Fatah was unquestionaly the preeminent organization in the Quwat Mushtarika, and the only group capable of even attempting to impose any discipline on Amal's adversaries. The significant, if transitory, importance of a relationship with Fatah was illustrated in late March 1980, when bloody street battles erupted in Beirut between Amal on the one side, and the Jabhat Arabiyya and the Popular Nasserite Organization on the other side. The fighting, which left twenty-seven dead, so alarmed Yasir Arafat (leader of Fatah and chairman of the PLO Executive Committee) that he interrupted the Fourth Fatah Congress, then in progress in Damascus, and returned to Beirut to mediate the conflict.

By the summer of 1980, two tendencies with respect to the armed Palestinian presence in Lebanon were discernible within Harakat Amal. The more moderate tendency, stemming from sympathy for the Palestinian cause and a recognition that the Palestinian presence was not likely to be soon terminated by a peaceful solution, held that Amal's enemies were those who affiliated with anti-Shi'a governments (viz., Iraq and Libya). Fatah, for those espousing this point of view, was not only a useful *wasita* but a worthy ally of Amal. The second tendency, which even in 1980 clearly represented the mainstream, held the Palestinians and *all* foreign interlopers responsible for the continuing troubles in Lebanon. According to the latter point of view, any relationship with Fatah (or any fedayeen organization for that matter) was merely instrumental and transitory.

Despite the public posturing of Amal officials and the staunchly pro-fedayeen line of the movement's weekly organ, *Amal*, the delicate entente between Amal and Fatah steadily deteriorated between 1980 and 1982. Clashes occurred with increasing regularity, and all but the pretense of amity vanished. While Fatah attempted to maintain a modicum of control over the movement through local joint security committees (which in practice it dominated) and various forms of pressure and intimidation, the movement's geographic disperson, diffuse leadership, and rapidly growing support made such attempts increasingly ineffective.

One corollary of the movement's hidden agenda bears noting at this point: the consistent public support that it has declared for the deployment of the Lebanese army throughout Lebanon. While the National Movement and the Lebanese Front represented alternative legitimacy structures, Amal committed itself to the reestablishment of the central government's authority—an essentially conservative position that well served the interests of a constituency that sought security and a fair share of political rewards. Amal's stand on the deployment of the army did not endear it to its erstwhile allies who continued to see the army as a Maronite-dominated force that was opposed by definition to the reformist National Movement (and its Palestinian allies).[63] Thus, Amal's support of the army further emphasized its antithetical position from the Quwat Mushtarika, and it also fed suspicion that the movement (or significant parts of it) was no more than a stalking horse for the army's intelligence agency, the Deuxième Bureau. (While Amal's support certainly warmed some hearts in the Lebanese army, it is not clear that the military has in any way directed or buttressed Amal.)

In addition to supporting the army, the movement sought to associate itself with any program or institution that symbolized legitimate government in Lebanon. Furthermore, it took every opportunity to compel the government to extend its authority. As previously noted, one consistent focus of Amal has been the governmental neglect suffered by those living in the South. A palpable symbol of that neglect has been the Majlis al-Junub (Council of the South). Chartered in 1970 to foster economic development, the council has languished, corruption ridden. Amal made the council a constant target for criticism and protest, and in September 1980, occupied the council offices in Saida and prevented its employees from entering the building. Simultaneously, Nabih Berri announced a series of demands, including the more timely and adequate compensation of those who had been displaced or had suffered property damage due to hostilities. The movement threatened to take over the council if its demands were not met.[64] It is hard to conceive that a more popular or politically lucrative target could have been chosen. By attacking the Majlis al-Junub, Amal raised an issue of widespread concern, forced the government to take a keener interest in the welfare of its citizens, and identified itself with a legitimate governmental function.

While it is beyond the scope of this paper to explore fully Harakat Amal's relationship with Syria, it should be acknowledged that the relationship has been close indeed. Amal's weapons admittedly were supplied "via" Syria,[65] and the Syrians may have played a role in training Amal militiamen. Nabih Berri affirmed his movement's relationship with Syria in February 1982, when in an enunciation of Amal's goals, he included: "The definition of special military, security, economic and cultural realations between Lebanon and Syria, and the specification of Israel as Lebanon's arch-enemy."[66]

The Amal-Syria relationship served as yet another proof of the danger that Amal represented for the Quwat Mushtarika. Certainly since the June 1976 Syrian intervention on the side of the Lebanese Front, the relationship between the PLO and its ally with Syria has been frosty to say the least.[67] It should be recalled that the Imam Al-Sadr broke with the National Movement in 1976 when he supported the Syrian intervention. While documentation is unavailable, it is not unreasonable to assume tht Amal was, to a degree at least, a means by which Hafez al-Assad could temper the actions of those groups that he could not directly control. (The strongest fedayeen presence was south of the Israeli-delimited red line, where Syrian forces were excluded.)

In early 1982, widespread skirmishes broke out in a number of southern villages, and then in April fighting between Amal and its adversaries erupted in Beirut and in sixteen southern villages. According to an Amal account, elements belonging to or aligned to Fatah, conducted a ten-hour bombardment of the Technical Institute in Burj ash-Shimali during the April fighting.[68] These serious clashes represented an important watershed for several reasons: When the fighting was brought to a halt, Amal forces—for the first time—remained in control of disputed villages.[69] Significantly, under the auspices of the Higher Coordination Committee (consisting of representatives from the PLO, National Movement, Harakat Amal, and Syria) it was agreed that the PLO "should henceforth not involve itself in Lebanese internal security matters" but should concentrate on "strategic security."

In the months preceding the Israeli invasion, the contradictions separating

the Quwat Mushtarika from Amal had become highly salient. The character of
the relationship was well illustrated by the contrasting public statements of
Salah Khalaf (*nom de guerre*, Abu Iyad; usually identified as the second in
command in al-Fatah) and the leading Shi'a cleric, the Imam Muhammad
Mahdi Shams ad-Din. When Salah Khalaf was asked in December 1981 about
Fatah's relationshiup with Amal, he replied, ''in fact, there is no conflict between the resistence and the Amal movement. Indeed relations are good.''[70]
Commenting on the same subject, just two months later, Khalaf had clearly
lost his patience with Amal:

> We address our brothers in the Amal movement, not the schemers in Amal, but
> the brother nationalist whom we know take the initiative in the Amal movement
> and participate in the joint command and the joint forces in the South so that we
> can prevent all evil elements and schemers in various areas from scheming in
> southern Lebanon. We reaffirm that we are concerned about the Amal move-
> ment . . . so that they will be with us in the same trench, within one joint com-
> mand.[71]

Following the April fighting, Shams ad-Din, who is deputy chairman of the
Higher Shi'a Council (Musa al-Sadr is chairman until he reaches the age of 65
in 1993), offered his first public criticism of the fedayeen and the National
Movement. His strongly worded statement, which follows, was widely interpreted as an important hardening of the Amal position:

> The Higher Shi'a Council urgently asks *those responsible in the Palestinian re-
> sistance and the Nationalist Movement* to stop the shelling of the villages imme-
> diately, to pull the gunmen out of them and to withdraw the weapons directed at
> them. The continuation of this situation portends grave consequences for the
> entire Arab situation. The people of the South are now facing Arab bullets,
> which are supposed to be directed at Israel, and are being displaced from their
> homes not by Israelis but by fellow Arabs [emphasis added].[72]

Even Nabih Berri, who is reknowned for his conciliatory rhetoric,[73] did not
hesitate to contradict the PLO leadership claims that Palestinians were not involved in the April clashes.[74]

The Public Agenda

The public agenda espoused by Harakat Amal has had an immediate, literally conservative dimension and a long-range, reformist dimension. The
movement's immediate goals, as alluded to above, have been to preserve the
unity of Lebanon and reimpose state authority and sovereignty throughout the
country.[75] Consistent with these goals, the movement has opposed any attempt to proliferate alternative governmental structures. Nabih Berri even
suggested that the heavy fighting of April 1982 was precipitated by the National Movement's attempt to elect ''local councils'' in Ras Beirut (West

Beirut). The election of local councils was seen by Amal as a "form of autonomy" that might be preliminary to the partition of Lebanon.[76]

While the immediate goals have been conservative, the longer-term prescriptions promoted by the movement amount to changing the criterion—confessional identity—by which political rewards are allocated. Nabih Berri has argued that confessionalism has precluded the development of a Lebanese nationality and has been the root cause of the country's travails.[77]

> This [confessional] hallucination we have in our minds has made us behave like tribes instead of like people of one country. The 1943 National Pact that we created is a partitionist pact. It helped us to build a farm, not a country . . . I say this Pact is the root of all of our troubles.[78]

> Because here the economic and employment competition is built on a purely sectarian basis. Sectarianism is imposed on us. They are making us wear turbans and priests' robes and forcing us to think confessional.[79]

Until early 1982, the movement called for the abolition of confessionalism "from the top of the pyramid to its base," [80] excepting the top three political positions and them only long enough to show that deconfessionalism was working. By February 1982, the position had softened considerably, although deconfessionalism was still to be the ultimate goal. "The abolition of the sectarianism must at least start in the army and in education, in the hope that this will lead to the total abolition of political secretarianism in Lebanon eventually." [81]

At first glance, the position publicized by Berri is not complementary to the collective interests of the Shi'a community, which would stand to benefit from a reallocation of political positions and rewards according to their share of the demographic pie. On closer examination, two factors justify the call for jettisoning (albeit slowly) confessionalism. Most important, it was the proliferation of parochial sectarian interests that, according to one interpretation, made the civil war possible and thwarted the cessation of violence. Berri's deputy, Hasan Hashim, has asserted that the outside powers—especially the East and West military camps—were able to exploit secretarianism in furtherance of their aim to control the Palestinian revolution. Hashim notes:

> Lebanon is a victim of the dirty political game laid out by the Eastern and Western Camps.

> All of the organizations active on the Lebanese state (except Harakat Amal) were connected and affiliated toward one of the Arab countries or an outside foreign power, and all of these groups and organizations were deeply and thickly involved in Lebanon and in the developments which took place in it.[82]

Thus, to leave the Lebanese system unchanged is to maintain its keen vulnerability to meddling by outside powers. There is one other aspect to this position: the opinion, voiced from time to time in the movement's weekly, that the Shi'as were the only sect lacking an outside sponsor and that they suffered accordingly.[83]

Deconfessionalizing Lebanese politics is obviously a profoundly difficult matter, and one that requires the support of precisely those who stand to lose the most if it is to be implemented. Less radical reforms, which preserve confessional politics but recognize Shi'a claims through the reallocation of political privileges, may well satisfy an assertive Shi'a community. As Fuad Khuri has put it, the formula (i.e., the 1943 National Covenant) would be preserved, but the equation by which political roles have been distributed would be changed to reflect new realities.[84] While definitive evidence is naturally absent, there is certainly room to conjecture that Amal might be aiming at an important revision of the political equation. Specifically, Berri and others in the movement have made statements that betoken a blurring of sectarian distributions between Sunnis and Shi'as. By minimizing or even denying differences between the two sects, the way may be opening for Shi'a claims to Muslim (i.e., Sunni) seats of power (viz., the premiership). For example, speaking in the wake of the Israeli invasion, Berri observed:

> There is one Muslim community in Lebanon, and there are no differences. Regrettably, however, we still have the mentality of 1943, and I dread to say the mentality of 1864. I say it is absolutely impossible to disregard any side in the Lebanese arena. The Muslim community in Lebanon constitutes half of the population of Lebanon and even more, and it has its rights. It has discharged many duties. I add that our Christian brothers cannot be dispensed with or replaced, as a cohesive national unity, we must rise with Lebanon from a Lebanese premise and not from a sectarian premise.[85]

Although the Amal position has expressly excluded federalist or confederalist solutions,[86] as the Lebanese Front has proposed from time to time,[87] the movement has been careful not to exclude the discussion of any political program. In short, it has striven to project a conciliatory pose that makes it a natural interlocutor. Berri has stated that any changes that are undertaken should result from a dialogue between "all active forces in Lebanon without exception."[88] Given the movement's troubled relations with the PLO, its strong relationship with Syria, and its promotion of Lebanese nationalism, its presence in any government will both solve problems for the Maronites and salve any misgivings they might have about power-sharing arrangements with the Shi'as.

In discussing a movement that venerated Imam Musa al-Sadr, it is appropriate to note that observers often found Imam Musa's intentions elusive. As one writer put it, "No one could specify where he stood politically."[89] One great admirer of the Imam, whose relationship began over twenty years ago, often remarked that "Imam Musa was a pragmatist not an ideologue." Thus we probably should not be surprised to find that Imam Musa's political heirs will be perfectly capable of adapting to any political solution that accommodates their interests.

Notes

"AMAL" is also an acronyn for Afwaj al-Muqawimah al-Lubnaniyah—the Lebanese Resistance Detachments. However, in my many contacts with members of the movement I have always heard "Amal" used to denote hope.

This study is dedicated to Muhammed 'Aqil Salum, a poor, but not simple villager from a decrepit village in the South, who was murdered in November 1980 after being abducted by thugs working for Sa'ad Haddad. Salum had more courage than most of us.

The opinions presented in this paper are those of the author and should not be construed to represent the position of the U.S. Military Academy or any other institution, organization, or agency of the United States government. The author especially wishes to thank Richard Cottam, Nikola Schahgaldian, and George Irani for their thoughtful comments and criticisms. Special thanks also to J.C. Hurewitz for the opportunity to present an early version of this chapter at the Middle East Center, Columbia University, in December 1981.

This is a slightly altered version of a paper prepared for delivery at the annual meeting of the American Political Science Association, Denver, September 2-5, 1982.

1. One measure of the marginality of the Shi'as is the fact that most political studies written prior to the Civil War almost totally ignored them. The following two books are notable exceptions: Michael C. Hudson, *The Precarious Republic: Political Modernization in Lebanon* (New York: Random House, 1968); and David R. Smock and Audrey C. Smock, *The Politics of Pluralism: A Comparative Study of Lebanon and Ghana* (New York: Elsevier, 1975).
2. Useful population estimates may be found in: Joseph Chamie, "The Lebanese Civil War: An Investigation into the Causes," *World Affairs* 139 (Winter 1976/1977): 171-88; and Riad B. Tabbarah, "Background to the Lebanese Conflict," *International Journal of Comparative Sociology* 20, nos. 1-2 (1980): 101-21.
3. Chamie, "Lebanese Civil War," p. 179.
4. Hudson, *Precarious Republic*, p. 79.
5. Tabbarah, "Background to the Lebanese Conflict," p. 118.
6. Husan Sharif, "South Lebanon: Its History and Geopolitics," in *South Lebanon*, ed. Elaine Hagopian and Samih Farsoun (Detroit: Association of Arab-American University Graduates, August 1978), pp. 10-11.
7. Ibid., p. 11.
8. Karl W. Deutsch, "Social Mobilization and Political Development," *American Political Science Review* 55 (September 1961): 493-514.
9. Ibid., p. 493.
10. Ibid., pp. 497-98.
11. See Hudson, *Precarious Republic*, esp. pp. 53-86.
12. For a useful discussion of Deutsch's position on assimilation versus dissimilation, see Walker Connor's important article: "Nation-Building or Nation-Destroying?" *World Politics* 24 (1972): 319-55, esp. pp. 321-28.
13. Deutsch, "Social Mobilization," p. 501. Also see Deutsch, *Politics and Government: How People Decide Their Fate*, 2d ed. (Boston: Houghton Mufflin, 1974),

p. 544, where he notes: "Social mobilization makes people more available for change. It does so by inducing them or teaching them to change their residence, their occuptions, their communications, their associates, and their outlook and imagination. It gives rise to new needs, new aspirations, new demands and capabilities. *But all these new patterns of behavior may disunite a population or unite it. They can make people more similar or more different. They may produce cooperation or strife, integration or succession*" (italics added).

14. I am construing political participation in a wide sense, following the usage of Myron Weiner, who defines it as follows: "Any voluntary action, successful or unsuccessful, organized or unorganized, episodic or continuous, employing legitimate or illegitimate methods intended to influence the choice of public policies, the administration of public affairs, or the choice of political leaders at any level of government local or national." "Political Participation," in *Crisis and Sequences in Political Development*, ed. Leonard Binder et al. (Princeton University Press, 1971), pp. 159-204, at p. 164.

15. Hudson, *Precarious Republic*, p. 21.

16. On the preservation of sectarian identity in Beirut, see: Fuad I. Khuri, "The Social Dynamics of the 1975-1977 War in Lebanon," *Armed Forces and Society* 7 (Spring 1981): 383-408; Khuri, "A Comparative Study of Migration Patterns in Two Lebanese Villages," *Human Organization* 26, no. 4 (1967). See also: Smock, *Politics of Pluralism*, p. 93.

17. Hudson, *Precarious Republic*, p. 61.

18. Khuri, "Social Dynamics of the War," p. 392.

19. For an instructive (and controversial) fictional treatment of a young Shi'a woman's attempt to "escape" from her village and her sect, see: Tawfig Yusuf Awwad, *Death in Beirut*, trans. Leslie McLoughlin (London: Heinemann, 1976).

20. Daniel Lerner, *The Passing of Traditional Society: Modernizing the Middle East* (New York: Free Press, 1958), p. 61.

21. Deutsch, "Social Mobilization," pp. 497-98.

22. Ibid., p. 499.

23. Samuel P. Huntington, *Political Order in Changing Societies* (New Haven: Yale University Press, 1968), p. 47.

24. Fuad I. Khuri, *From Village to Suburb: Order and Change in Greater Beirut* (Chicago: University of Chicago Press, 1975), p. 8.

25. Hudson, *Precarious Republic*, pp. 31-32.

26. Before the Civil War began in 1975, the political loyalty of the Shi'a community in the South was fragmented. In addition to al-Sadr, the principal contenders were Kamal al-As'ad, the scion of a famous Shi'a *za' im*; the Khalil family of Tyre; and various political parties, including the several Baath factions, Communists, Syrian Social Nationalist party, and a few Nasserist groups.

27. Biographical data have been extracted from: *al-Sadr!?* (Beirut: Dar al-Khalud, 1979) pp. 11-17.

28. Raphael Calis, "The Shiite Pimpernel," *Middle East*, November 1978, p. 52.

29. Smock, *Politics of Pluralism*, p. 141.

30. Sharif, "South Lebanon," p. 18. Many Lebanese refer to the council as the Majlis al-Juyub (the Council of the Pockets) in recognition of the reputation for bribery and illegal diversions of funds. As will be noted below, the council became an important target for Amal activism in 1980.

31. "Rivalry to Lead the Shi'a in Lebanon," *Arab World Weekly* (Beirut), February 16, 1974, p. 11.

32. Calis, "Shiite Pimpernel," p. 53.
33. Ibid.
34. Kamal S. Salibi, *Crossroads to Civil War: Lebanon 1958-1976* (Delmar, NY: Caravan Books, 1976), p. 78.
35. Ibid., p. 119.
36. The precise dimensions of the relationship with Syria are difficult to discern. My impression is that conjecture to the effect that the relationship is based on sectarian affinities is incorrect. While Hafez al-As'ad does belong to the Alawi sect that some consider to be an offshoot of the Shi'a, I believe that the basis of the relationship is pragmatic. Syria's proximity (one Amal official said: "You can ignore history but not geography") and utility as an ally explain the ties.
37. Strictly speaking, the ALF (Jabhat Arabiyya) is a constituent group in the PLO, and its Lebanese counterpart is the Iraqi faction of the Baath party; however, there were in fact Lebanese in both segments, and as a result, most Lebanese do not distinguish between the two.
   The authenticity of Shi'a communism is—prudently—treated with skepticism in Salibi, *Crossroads to Civil War*, p. 143.
38. John Kifner estimates that $25 million a month flows into Lebanon to support the various militias. "Life Among the Ruins in Beirut," *New York Times Magazine*, December 6, 1981, p. 162. Amal officials claim that their members are not paid and, in fact, that they pay monthly dues (from £L 5-10 upward.) While the truth of this claim may be questioned, I do know that many rank-and-file members take great pride in their lack of remuneration.
39. The Kata'ib, the Maronite militia commanded by Bashir Gemayel, is sometimes referred to as the Phalange.
   John Bulloch argues that the August 6, 1976, fall of the Nabaa suburb of Beirut to the Kata'ib was facilitated by al-Sadr's defection (in league with his adversary Kamal al-As'ad) to the Syrians, who were at that time allied with the Kata'ib. See: *Death of a Country: The Civil War in Lebanon* (London: Weidenfeld and Nicolson, 1977), pp. 172-73.
40. Calis, "Shiite Pimpernel," p. 54.
41. Quoted in the *Jerusalem Post*, March 25, 1981.
42. *Monday Morning* (Beirut), December 22-28, 1980, p. 13.
43. Smock, *Politics of Pluralism*, p. 142; and Salibi, *Crossroads to Civil War*, pp. 63-64.
44. For a recent recounting, see; David K. Shipler, "Lebanese Tell of Anguish of Living Under the P.L.O.," *New York Times*, July 25, 1982.
45. See: Walid Khalidi, *Conflict and Violence in Lebanon: Confrontation in the Middle East* (Cambridge: Harvard University, Center for International Affairs, 1979), pp. 115-16.
46. Private communication.
47. *al-Sadr!?*, pp. 61-62. The documentation reproduced in *al-Sadr!?* supports the claims of the Imam's followers.
48. A report of September 9, 1980, indicated that al-Sadr was being held in a Libyan military camp near the Algerian border. See: *New York Times*, September 10, 1980.
49. Private communication.
50. *Christian Science Monitor*, April 17, 1978.
51. *L'Orient-Le Jour*, September 16, 1980.
52. Lydia Georgi, interview with Nabih Berri, *Monday Morning* (Beirut), February

1-7, 1982, pp. 14-25; trans. and reprinted by Foreign Broadcast Information Service, *Daily Report-Middle East and Africa*, February 10, 1982, pp. G1-G6, at p. G4. Foreign Broadcast Information Service is hereafter referred to as FBIS. Berri has served since early 1980 as the chairman of the Amal Command Council. He is a lawyer whose family home is in Tibneen, a major town in the South.

53. For example, see: John Yemma, "Lebanon's Shiite Muslims Flex Their Military Muscles," *Christian Science Monitor*, January 12, 1982; Thomas L. Friedman, "One Civil War Is Over, Others Fast Multiply," *New York Times*, May 23, 1982; "The Rise of Yet Another Enemy for the Palestinians," *Economist*, May 1, 1972, p. 65; and Scheherezade Faramarzi, "Shiites Get Some Hope: New Force Arises in Lebanon," *Sunday Record* (Middletown, NY), February 28, 1982. Cf. Augustus Richard Norton, "Lebanon's Shiites," *New York Times*, April 16, 1982.

54. Nabih Berri interview, February 1-7, 1982, p. G2.

55. Of course, for many villagers, the best politics was no politics at all, a feeling that is well summed up in the folk proverb *"Ra'ih al-Baqir Ahsan Min Siyasat al-Bashar"* (The idea of a cow is preferable to the politics of the people).

56. For descriptions of the situation in Lebanon circa 1981 and 1982, see: Augustus Richard Norton, "Lebanon's Shifting Political Landscape," *New Leader*, March 8, 1983, pp. 8-9; idem, "The Violent Work of Politics in Lebanon," *Wall Street Journal*, March 18, 1982; and William Haddad, "Divided Lebanon," *Current History*, January 1982, pp. 30-35.

57. Lest the wrong impression be given, it should be noted that members of the movement were not reluctant to take offensive action when possible. For example, on February 18, 1981, an attempt was made to kidnap a cleric, Imam Ahmad Shawkey al-Amin of Majdal Silm, who opposed Amal. In Beirut, Amal was thought to have initiated hostilities on a number of occasions.

58. It would be misleading not to note that while the parties of the left were being clearly overshadowed by Amal within the Shi'a community, successful recruiting activities among the Shi'as by the Lebanese Communist party, for example, continued at least through 1981.

59. *Le Matin* (Paris), May 28, 1982.

60. For the positions of various groups and factions, see: *Monday Morning*, December 22-28, 1980; December 29, 1980-January 12-18, 1981; January 19-25, 1981; January 26-February 1, 1981.

61. For a personal account of the Civil War, especially in Beirut, see: Lina Mikdadi Tabbara, *Survival in Beirut: A Diary of Civil War*, trans. Nadia Hijab (London: Onyx Press, 1979).

62. It was only in early 1982 that the public statements of Amal officials began to match private perceptions.

63. Figures on the confessional profile of the Lebanese Armed Forces are closely held, and even authoritative estimates are unavailable to my knowledge. My impression is that officer recruitment is being carried out along strict confessional lines, with a 50-50 split between Muslims and Christians, with appropriate proportional allocations for each of Lebanon's seventeen recognized sects. Within the army there is an ongoing program of integration to eliminate units that are wholly of one sect. However, as one American University of Beirut professor noted, it is hard to integrate the military when the larger society remains unintegrated.

64. *An-Nahar*, September 18, 1980.

65. Nabih Berri interview, February 1-7, 1982, p. G2.

66. Ibid.

67. See: Abu Iyad (Salah Khalaf), with Eric Rouleau, *My Home, My Land: A Narrative of the Palestinian Struggle*, trans. Linda Butler Koseoglu (New York: Times Books, 1981), passim.

68. Private communication.

69. *Economist*, May 1, 1982, p. 65.

70. *Al-Watan* (Kuwait), November 25, 1981.

71. From a speech by Salah Khalaf, broadcase by the Voice of Palestine, trans. and reprinted by FBIS, February 4, 1982, p. G3.

72. Interview with Shaykh Muhammad Mahdi Shams al-Din, *An-Nahar al-Arabi wa al-Dawli*, May 24-30, 1982, pp. 13-15, trans. and reprinted by FBIS, June 3, 1982, p. G2.

73. A number of Amal officials, among them moderates, were critical of Berri's penchant for equivocation. One moderate leader stated that he in fact preferred Husayn Husayni, Berri's predecessor, because Husayni was a "yes or no man; he was inflexible," whereas lawyer Berri was "too much the attorney." (Private interview.)

74. See: Interview with Nabih Berri, *Monday Morning*, May 10-16, 1982, pp. 14-19, trans. and reprinted by FBIS, May 25, 1982, p. G3.

75. Ibid., p. G4.

76. Nabih Berri interview, May 10-16, 1982, p. G4.

77. Berri's analysis is certainly shared by a number of long-time observers, including Michael Hudson: "The confessional system itself—as the embodiment of a consociational model—was the root of the problem." ("The Lebanese Crisis: The Limits of Consociational Democracy," *Journal of Palestine Studies* 5, nos. 3-4 (Spring/Summer 1976): 114.

78. Lydia Georgi, "The 'New Lebanon' File—Part 6: Amal Movement: The Myth of Pluralism," *Monday Morning*, January 26-February 1, 1981.

79. Ibid., p. 23.

80. Ibid.

81. Nabih Berri interview, February 1-7, 1982, p. G2.

82. Interview with Hasan Hashim, *Amal*, April 17, 1981, p. 8.

83. See, for example, an interesting commentary by an Amal writer on an article that appeared in the Kata'ib organ, *al-Amal*, the subject of which was Harakat Amal. *Amal*, April 17, 1981, pp. 6-7.

84. Khuri, "Social Dynamics of the War in Lebanon," pp. 393-95.

85. From a program broadcast by the Beirut Domestic Service, July 19, 1982, trans. and reprinted in FBIS, July 20, 1982, p. G2.

86. See Berri's comments in: *An-Nahar al-Arabi wa al-Dawli*, April 20-25, 1981, pp. 10-11.

87. See ibid. passim, and note 60.

88. Quoted in Georgi, "New Lebanon," p. 26.

89. Calis, "Shiite Pimpernel," p. 54.

About the Contributors

Myron J. Aronoff is professor of political science at Rutgers University. He received his Ph.D. in anthropology from Manchester University and his Ph.D. in political science from U.C.L.A. His major publications include *Frontiertown: The Politics of Community Building in Israel* and *Power and Ritual in the Israeli Labor Party: A Study in Political Anthropology.* He is the editor of the *Political Anthropology Series* and *Freedom and Constraint: A Memorial Tribute to Max Gluckman.* His major theoretical interest is in the relationship between culture and politics.

Eliezer Don-Yehiya is chairman of the Department of Political Studies at Bar-Ilan University, Israel. He is the author of numerous articles on religious Zionist history and Israeli politics, and co-author, with Charles S. Liebman, of *Piety and Politics: Religion and Politics in Israel* and *The Civil Religion in Israel* (1983).

Jerrold D. Green is assistant professor of political science and a member of the Center of Near Eastern and North African Studies at the University of Michigan. He has recently spent a year in Egypt, where he pursued research on Egyptian bureaucratic recruitment, as a Fulbright scholar and a Fellow of the American Research Center in Egypt. His most recent book is *Revolution in Iran: The Politics of Countermobilization* (1982).

Irving Louis Horowitz is Hannah Arendt distinguished professor of sociology and political science at Rutgers University. He is the author of numerous works in political sociology, among them *Foundations of Political Sociology* (1972); *Ideology and Utopia in the United States* (1976); *Beyond Empire and Revolution* (1982); and with Seymour Martin Lipset, *Dialogues on American Politics* (1978). He is editor-in-chief of *Transaction/SOCIETY* and founding editor of *Studies in Comparative International Development.*

Charles S. Liebman is professor of political studies at Bar-Ilan University, Israel. He is the author of numerous articles and books on Jewish sociology and religion and politics, including *The Ambivalent American Jew: Pressure without Sanctions* and *Influence of World Jewry on Israeli Policy*. His most recent book is *The Civil Religion of Israel* (1983), co-authored with Eliezer Don-Yehiya.

Wilson Carey McWilliams is professor of political science at Rutgers University. He is the author of *The Idea of Fraternity in America* and editor of *Worldview*, a journal of religion and international affairs.

Augustus Richard Norton is assistant professor in the Department of Social Sciences, U.S. Military Academy, West Point. He graduated with honors from the University of Miami and is currently a doctoral candidate in political science at the University of Chicago. He is the author of numerous articles and books, including *International Terrorism* and *Studies in Nuclear Terrorism*. He is continuing his research on the Shi'as in Lebanon.

Index

Compiled by Saliba Sarsar.